"Terence Lester's story is a powerful testament to the resilience of the human spirit and the transformative power of purpose."
Jacqulyne Horbrook, CEO of Black Christian Influencers

"Raw, unfiltered, and deeply personal, yet it exposes a larger truth about resilience and the fight against racism. This isn't just one man's journey; it's a call to action for all of us."
C. J. Stewart, transformational coach and former MLB player

"More than just a memoir; it's a roadmap for anyone who has ever felt marginalized, overlooked, or counted out."
Elizabeth Rosner, Nonviolence365® trainer at The King Center

"A powerful testament to the resilience of the human spirit and the urgent need for educational equity. . . . This book is not just inspiring—it's necessary."
Ryan Wilson, CEO and cofounder of The Gathering Spot

"Dr. Terence Lester is a leading voice in making us consider and reconsider our perspective and feeling about those who are unhoused."
Michael Simanga, assistant professor of Africana studies at Morehouse College

"Terence Lester uses his story to not only help us better understand our society but also to enter into the work of tending to our wounds."
Joel Edward Goza, author of *Rebirth of a Nation*

"This book is both a challenge to dismantle barriers to human flourishing and a stunning testament to what becomes possible when we create spaces where roses can break through concrete."
Jonathan Merritt, author of *Learning to Speak God from Scratch*

"As a Black woman who's often felt invisible, I see myself in Lester's story. This book is more than inspiration—it's a battery for the heart, charging you to believe beyond your beginnings."
Cierra Fly Bobo, founder of FLY Life Inc.

"By connecting trauma, policy, and poverty, Lester emphasizes the importance of combating educational injustice and unjust policies through community, mentorship, scholarship, and above all, love."
Rachael Wade, founder of Olive Us

"With unflinching honesty and hard-earned wisdom, the author explores the unique challenges faced within the Black community and how systemic barriers impact educational trajectories."
Monica P. Lester, licensed clinical social worker and therapist

"Lester's insights are a beautiful example of the powerful transformation that takes place when communities come together to address social inequities, making all things possible with God."
Antonio Mejico, associate dean for the division of social work at California Baptist University

"Dr. Terence Lester has woven together the intersections of history, systemic injustice in education, and his powerful story to provide an essential pedagogical resource for teachers and professors in America."
Rohadi Nagassar, author of *When We Belong*

"Dr. Terence Lester, my father, uses his voice to lead with purpose. He not only speaks up but also challenges others to grow through education."
Zion Lester, community leader and coauthor of *Zion Learns to See*

"This book is essential reading for educators, policymakers, faith leaders, and anyone who believes in the transformative power of equity and opportunity."
Lamar Hardwick, author of *How Ableism Fuels Racism*

"Drawing from thorough research, Lester expertly educates readers on the pervasive impact of trauma, racism, poverty, and systemic injustices that hinder individuals from achieving their full potential."
Monica DiCristina, therapist and author of *Your Pain Has a Name*

"This book doesn't shout; it invites, holding up a light to the parts of our society and ourselves that are often purposefully overlooked."
Bethny Ricks, author of *Face Forward* and *An Inconvenient Journey*

"This book is a comeback story that inspires, equips, and educates others on the importance of Black and Brown scholarship. With the state of education in the United States today, this book is a clarion call for us all."
Jefferson J. Jones, founder of Surge Ministries and cofounder of The Healing Project

"A resource that will spark meaningful conversation in any classroom, book club, faith context, social justice, or professional setting."
Gina A. S. Robinson, racial justice and unity in diversity program officer for Wayfarer Foundation

"Dr. Terence Lester is a national treasure . . . his book on educational injustice will inspire us all to reflect on our own struggles and find ways to serve people who are disadvantaged in whatever ways we can."
Stewart Burns, historian and Martin Luther King Jr. scholar

"Terence's example of not giving up, even when it would have been easier to quit, shows the strength of his 'why' and the heart behind his work."
Evan Dougoud, president and founder of BeHeard Movement

"This book is simultaneously a blueprint and balm for anyone committed to breaking generational chains and growing roses in concrete."
Ray James, head of school at The Boyce L. Ansley School

"Terence Lester is a gift to the church and to the world. This is his story–a story of resilience, faith, and resurrection. . . . Read it, share it, and let it inspire you to never give up on yourself or anybody else."
Shane Claiborne, cofounder of Red Letter Christians

FROM

DROPOUT

TO

DOCTORATE

BREAKING THE CHAINS OF
EDUCATIONAL INJUSTICE

TERENCE LESTER, PhD

FOREWORD BY JEMAR TISBY

ivp

An imprint of InterVarsity Press
Downers Grove, Illinois

InterVarsity Press
P.O. Box 1400 | Downers Grove, IL 60515-1426
ivpress.com | email@ivpress.com

InterVarsity Press® is the publishing division of InterVarsity Christian Fellowship/USA®. For more information, visit intervarsity.org.

All Scripture quotations, unless otherwise indicated, are taken from The Holy Bible, New International Version®, NIV®. Copyright © 1973, 1978, 1984, 2011 by Biblica, Inc.™ Used by permission of Zondervan. All rights reserved worldwide. www.zondervan.com. The "NIV" and "New International Version" are trademarks registered in the United States Patent and Trademark Office by Biblica, Inc.™

While any stories in this book are true, some names and identifying information may have been changed to protect the privacy of individuals.

Photos by Terence Lester and Dani Andujo Guerra used with permission.

Published in association with The Bindery Agency, www.TheBinderyAgency.com.

The publisher cannot verify the accuracy or functionality of website URLs used in this book beyond the date of publication.

Cover design: Faceout Studio, Molly von Borstel
Interior design: Daniel van Loon
Images: © CSA Images / Vetta via Getty Images, © jayk7 / Moment via Getty Images,
    © stockcam / E+ via Getty Images, © CHRISsadowski / E+ via Getty Images

ISBN 978-1-5140-1148-5 (print) | ISBN 978-1-5140-1149-2 (digital)

Printed in the United States of America ∞

Library of Congress Cataloging-in-Publication Data
A catalog record for this book is available from the Library of Congress.

31 30 29 28 27 26 25 | 12 11 10 9 8 7 6 5 4 3 2 1

**This book is dedicated to my father,
the late Tyrone Herman Lester.**

I will never forget you telling me in the hospital that I was one of the reasons you found faith in the Lord. I still play that audio clip when I need to be reminded that my struggle, our struggle, has not been in vain.

I remember our closeness these past seven years and what that meant to both of us. Not a day goes by that I don't reflect on how grateful I am to God for allowing us to find restoration and for how you became a close friend.

In your last moments before your transition, you fought long and hard. There were days that seemed so dark, but each day you allowed me to see your vulnerable side that was grounded in hope and resilience. Your vulnerability was a gift to me, and I am sure it was to my sisters. Vulnerability is hard but, when embraced, it allows us to see and appreciate the fragility of the human condition.

I love and miss you, Dad. The continuation of my dreams and the way I raise my children are connected to your legacy and honor the sacred memories I still hold near to my heart. Looking back, our struggle produced a friendship that had joy, faith in God, and forgiveness.

Throughout this book, I hope my stories of pain, forgiveness, and joy honor both my journey, your life, and the healing time we shared toward the end of your life. You always told me that no matter what comes our way, we must remain resilient and continue to be "forever forward." I believe you meant that we should never give up so long as we have breath in our bodies. That's what I hope to do with this book: continue to move forward with my dream and your legacy.

CONTENTS

FOREWORD

JEMAR TISBY

In my first career, I served as a sixth-grade science and social studies teacher in the Delta region of Arkansas. As a twenty-something novice teacher from the Midwest with a fresh undergraduate degree from the University of Notre Dame, I had no clue how different my world was from the students I was tasked to teach.

The middle school where I taught served students from fifth to eighth grade. According to standardized tests, on average, the incoming fifth grader was two grade levels behind in reading and one and a half grade levels behind in math. We focused on a college preparatory education, and when we asked students what they knew about college, they could only name the community college up the road. Nothing wrong with that, but they did not know about HBCUs or the network of publicly funded schools around the state or nearby in Mississippi and Tennessee. Recent census data indicated that just 14.3 percent of city residents held a bachelor's degree compared to 35 percent nationwide. College, for most of our students, was just a word and a remote reality meant for other people.

Our students also faced a complex of systemic issues that hindered their academic achievement. The Delta is cotton country. The frequent floods from the Mississippi River deposited rich sediment in the areas on both sides of the river. This, combined with the sweltering climate, made it perfect for growing the fluffy white fibers that made a handful of White men astronomically wealthy. The labor to cultivate all that cotton was forced onto enslaved people of African descent. After emancipation, some of those folks moved to the North and Midwest. Most stayed in the South. During the Jim Crow era, their children grew up to be sharecroppers, or worse, got caught in the carceral system and forced into "convict leasing" arrangements. Then came the mechanization of agriculture in the 1950s, and within a few years the farming that families had practiced for generations was no longer needed. The steady decline of factory jobs and industry left most of the remaining Black population in the Delta in crushing poverty.

The result was a community in which the Black population comprised the overwhelming majority of the town—75 percent. And most of those folks were poor. The most recent data states that the median household income in the city is $32,466 compared to $78,538 nationwide. The percent of people living at or below the poverty line is 32.4 percent compared to 11.1 percent across the country. All these sterile numbers took on personal dimensions in the form of the students who walked into my class each morning.

I'll always remember Jalen. He was a handsome boy. Deep, smooth, sable skin. Long, athletic arms and legs. A bright smile that made people feel like they just won the lottery every time he showed it. Some days Jalen would come to school buoyant, gregarious, and hilarious. Teachers and students both loved his presence because he made the entire atmosphere more effervescent. Other days he came in moping, moody, and inscrutable.

I had Jalen in my sixth-grade class, but it took years for me to realize the depth of issues he faced. A single mom with a volatile relationship with his father. Numerous siblings in a small house, which meant he never had a quiet moment alone to calm his nervous system. Previously undiagnosed learning disabilities that made traditional pedagogical approaches ineffective. All this and we expected him to come in uniform every day, with his homework done, ready to learn and participate.

I wish I had Dr. Terence Lester's book *From Dropout to Doctorate* when I was just starting as a teacher in the Delta. Hearing his story and understanding the personal and systemic effects of racism, poverty, and injustice would have immensely helped me to serve students like Jalen more effectively. I would have understood that many of our students had invisible burdens that they bravely shouldered each day. I would have had a much quicker road to becoming a more compassionate, skilled, and creative educator.

Thankfully, though, Dr. Lester has gifted us this book for this moment and for our posterity. He shares searing personal stories of tragedy and hardship that move the crisis in our educational system beyond statistics and into the realm of human impact. At the same time, he puts that doctorate to work. I found myself poring over his tables and illustrations, his definitions and theories. He adds academic ballast to his intimate narrative, so we come to understand not simply his individual story, but the historic and systemic forces at work that affect millions today.

Dr. Lester defied the odds. Black boys who come from environments like his aren't supposed to make it to adulthood, stay out of prison, start nonprofits to help people experiencing homelessness, raise healthy loving families, much less earn doctoral degrees. Not only was he able to accomplish all this—through a healthy community and faith in God, as he will be the first to tell you—but he now shares that hard-earned wisdom with us.

I am now a historian, and I have become acquainted with hundreds of people, both known and obscure, who have profoundly shaped our present-day realities. The historical figures I am most drawn to are the ones who have an undeniable moral credibility that they bring to the cause of justice. People like Frederick Douglass, who experienced enslavement and escaped to tell about it. People like Myrlie Evers-Williams, who held her dying husband in her arms after he was shot for their voting rights efforts. People like Fannie Lou Hamer, who grew up a poor sharecropper in the Mississippi delta just a short drive from where I taught. Dr. Lester has that kind of moral credibility. He is a person who has not simply studied educational and social hardships, he has endured them, survived them, and thrived as a result of the resilience he learned from them.

I lost track of Jalen after eighth grade. By that time, we had developed a high school, but his numerous discipline issues and struggling grades compelled his mother to put him in another school. I wish I had done better by him. I wish I had known then what I know now and what I see so much more clearly because of Dr. Lester. I hope Jalen, like Dr. Lester, is one of the exceptions— someone who overcame the personal and systemic forces conspiring to keep him stuck in place. The data says that is unlikely. But if I ever cross paths with Jalen again, whatever his circumstances, I will give him this book. I will tell him that it was written by someone just like him, who grew like a rose from concrete, and he can too.

WHEN ROSES GROW
FROM CONCRETE

Growing up in the early nineties, I listened to a lot of music. As I navigated childhood poverty and the impact of a home that ended in parental separation, music and poetry helped me cope with the pain, giving me a language I couldn't always articulate on my own.

One of my favorite artists was Tupac Shakur. Pac was complicated; his words could both inspire and upset you. I related to the side of him that was deep-thinking, reflective, and provided a critical analysis of the struggle of Black people. Songs like "Dear Mamma," "Keep Ya Head Up," "Brenda's Got a Baby," and "To Live & Die in LA" were deeply reflective of the Black struggle for survival during the late eighties and early nineties.

Knowing that Tupac wrote not just hip-hop but other forms of poetry gave me a chance to connect with him and add meaning to my reality. In 1999, MTV Books released Tupac's book of poetry, *The Rose That Grew from Concrete*, with poems that he had handwritten from 1989 to 1991.[1] The poems were discovered after his death. They talk about his struggle, the realities of the streets, the lack of support for impoverished communities, and his pain, fears, and hopes. The beginning of the poem that gives the book its title is loaded with depth and meaning, asking, had the reader heard of the rose that had grown "from a crack in the concrete?"

The poem is a metaphor that speaks to the beauty contained within people who have to navigate the harsh realities of poverty.

Yet it also reveals the systemic concrete-like layers that make it even harder for that beauty to grow. His words could even paint a powerful metaphor of a child who, by their impoverished circumstances, experiences more trauma even than some adults, yet still tries to do their best. That child may live in a food desert, suffer verbal or physical abuse by a family member, have to take care of their siblings while their one parent or guardian goes to work, have to deal with poverty and urban hassles, or have to choose between buying food and washing their clothes in the coin laundry.[2] The concrete may be their own body: sex-trafficked, exploited, experiencing homelessness, living in a motel room with five or more family members. It may be their mind: struggling with depression or exhaustion, too distracted and encumbered by pain to connect with schoolwork. It may be the foster care system: the state of having no family strong enough to care for them or no family at all. Whatever the story, some young person is that rose, trying to overcome the injustices created by the hard exterior of their environment.

I know. I was one of those roses.

I grew up in poverty on Campbellton Road in the city of Atlanta. As a teenager, I joined a street gang. I dropped out of school, and I experienced moments of homelessness—after choosing to leave home—and hopelessness. Many times, I didn't think I would make it.

In my mind, I can still see the unfinished roads because the local government wouldn't be quick to make repairs. The vacant lots. The Black businesses, holding on by a thread called community. The liquor stores and pawn shops, deep symbols of neglect and disinvestment, not to mention the school buildings that were never renovated when I was a child, leaving students with outdated textbooks and inadequate facilities. I can still hear the sounds of sirens and feel the fear of getting caught in the crossfire, which became part of daily life because of the hostile nature of trying to survive.

These circumstances and environments can lead to deep trauma in the life of a young person, young adult, or any adult trying to survive. Poverty, inadequate housing, a lack of guidance, and hopelessness all contribute to a deep sense of feeling stuck with the burden of nihilism. This type of environment requires immense resilience, grit, and a set of survival tactics that become second nature to any young person trying to navigate it all.

Even as a child, I had a deep understanding and intuition that education could give me the space to dream, escape, and imagine myself in places beyond my social context. But my environment had a more significant impact on my educational path than I would have wanted. Imagine journeying through such experiences while trying to produce good grades and maintain enough courage to get to school, sit in a classroom, and do schoolwork. The trauma from being raised in poverty makes it challenging to focus on learning when survival is the primary concern, let alone listen to a teacher teach about things that have nothing to do with your reality or existential experiences.

However, I want to preface my work in this book by saying that poverty does not mean less community, less brilliance, less courage or collective strength. In fact, many who navigate poverty exhibit extraordinary resilience, creativity, and solidarity in ways that often go unrecognized.

In another poem, "Government Assistance or My Soul," Tupac challenges the stereotypes that often stigmatize those faced with poverty and unemployment.[3] He makes it clear that not everyone who needs assistance from the government because they are poor is brought to that point because of personal failings; rather, they have been met with systemic conditions that contribute to their lack and suffering. Tupac's powerful poetic words shed light on both the physical and emotional toll it takes daily to survive and grow under harsh conditions. The words in the poem communicate how poverty attacks one's sense of self, altering how one sees the world and others.

I know this firsthand because I had my own struggles growing up in a single-parent home, seeing my mother work multiple jobs to take care of my sister and me. The trauma from family breakdown and poverty caused abuse, unhealthy communication, neglect, and other harmful traumas in my own life and the life of my family. My own encounters with trauma and poverty have given me a deeper understanding of the havoc they wreak on communities and lives, creating all types of emotional challenges that become nearly impossible to escape without proper support. It is a fact and reality that this happens more to Black children and children of color who are trying to find a way out of environments that have historical and systemic injustices tied to them.

The interplay of poverty and racial injustice introduces an additional layer of complexity to the struggle of someone navigating all this, often placing them at a significant disadvantage when it comes to educational achievement. It creates the type of barriers that uphold what I would call *educational injustice*. When I say *educational injustice*, I am talking about systemic barriers and inequities that disproportionately hinder Black children and children of color from historically marginalized communities, making it harder for them to flourish in school (K-12) and blocking their path to quality education and higher learning. These barriers make it harder for them to succeed and thrive like their peers who do not have to deal with systemic and social ills. Children raised with trauma and in poverty start from behind, long after the race has begun, and must navigate through fraught social and emotional landscapes. This burden is deeply rooted in a broader historical and systemic context that demands more understanding as we look at why access to higher education (that is, bachelor's degree, master's degree, and PhD programs) is harder for children of color, particularly children who are Black.

Poverty, trauma, and their effects can be long lasting for any child or adult trying to overcome them and can set a person up for failure—whether in getting a job, navigating a healthy family life, or pursuing academic achievement. Even if a person never plans to seek higher education, it is still important to feel safe enough to pursue whatever they want—to have equity meet them. That so many people never feel that kind of safety is due to systemic barriers, meticulously constructed over generations, that create what some scholars identify as transgenerational or multigenerational trauma: a phenomenon I discuss in depth in chapter two and give real life examples of throughout the book.[4]

I define systemic barriers as a set of hindrances, embedded obstacles, social challenges, and designed limitations that are socially constructed to hold back, oppress, or marginalize a vulnerable group of people from the resources and opportunities that might give them access to upward mobility. Consider the jelly-beans-in-a-jar test that hindered Black people from the political process and voting. Targeted policing and racial profiling. Vagrancy laws. Unequal education and health care. Or any number of other barriers that disadvantage a group of people. What drives these barriers are public policies that establish false social norms, mostly put in place by the people who hold power and can decide who those public policies will aid or disadvantage. These decisions structurally marginalize communities, placing a lid on potential for educational, social, and economic growth.

However, what we do not often talk about is how systemic barriers are deeply connected to trauma—and how this trauma itself can travel through generations, becoming emotional and social roadblocks. According to the mental health treatment facility A Place of HOPE, experiencing trauma as a child leaves lasting mental and emotional scars that extend beyond childhood, affecting people into adulthood. These experiences can make it hard to see the path ahead clearly, especially when it comes to having the right support system in place to access the academy beyond the K–12 experience.[5] Systemic injustice, a lack of access, and many other factors can hinder any Black young person from reaching their full potential academically. That is why there are not many PhDs that emerge from the concrete Tupac evokes, from neighborhoods that have higher concentrations of poverty and trauma or have been otherwise neglected. Indeed, it wasn't until I was fully grown that I met someone who held a doctorate outside of going to a medical doctor, and those doctors did not look like me or come from the type of environment that I emerged from.

As a child, my trauma inheritance affected me and my sense of my academic and educational potential in many ways.[6] Consider the type of public school I went to. At the time, before the newer homes and gated communities, it sat in an underfunded, impoverished neighborhood. Systemic policies result in fewer resources, underpaid teachers, and outdated buildings. These conditions limit the quality of education and the overall experience that students receive, limits that show up in the form of educational injustice. Meanwhile, the students often deal with significant generational trauma, such as family instability, economic burdens, and exposure to violence, which affects their ability to focus and succeed academically. Recognizing the impact of not just one's own localized trauma but that of one's forebears and broader community has helped me understand my own journey. Being trauma informed, community minded, and focused on healing can help educators and faith community leaders support students as they navigate the effects of such trauma and attempt to heal and obtain higher education.

GENERATIONAL TRAUMA AND EDUCATIONAL INEQUITY FRAMEWORK

Historical/ systemic oppression	Injustice/ policy	Poverty/ social conditions	Trauma/ barriers	Educational injustices/ challenges
Historical, systemic oppression and white supremacy initiate a cycle with long-lasting trauma effects and play a foundational role in shaping societal norms and institutions through their ideologies, directly impacting Africans brought to America and enslaved, and other communities of color. Systems and structures lead to the exclusion, discrimination, and mis-treatment of Black people and commu-nities of color in society, ultimately affecting educational outcomes. This influences injustices and policies that target specific marginalized communities.	Public policies have been weaponized by those in power who supported the mis-treatment, exclusion, and punishment of enslaved Africans through the use of power, policy, and legal institutions. This historical legacy continues to impact the descendants of those who endured chattel slavery, Black codes, vagrancy laws, Jim Crow, redlining, concentrated poverty, the War on Drugs, and many other systemic injustices that have specifically targeted Black and Brown communities. Rooted in oppressive ideologies, these policies have caused harm and have led to harsh living conditions that continue to affect communities today.	Policies, discrimination, and oppression have been leveraged to create harsh living conditions and concentrate poverty within Black and Brown communities, which has impacted access to housing, education, and other critical resources for upward mobility that impact overall wellness. These conditions have inflicted a lot of harm and social exclusion, and they have contributed to ongoing trauma within the Black community. This has led to further trauma and barriers.	The sustained social ills and living conditions, discrimination, and restricted access to equitable resources contribute to a trauma deeply rooted in the history of white supremacy and discriminatory policies. This trauma shows up as health issues, social and emotional heaviness that many carry in their bodies, and educational barriers. These factors collectively can hinder efforts to overcome these adverse social conditions which could directly impact and influence not-so-great educational outcomes. This could perpetuate cycles of suffering, injustice, and disparity in educational opportunities and accessing higher education.	Educational injustices and challenges faced by Black and Brown people are deeply intertwined with a cycle of trauma, historical oppression, injustice, generational poverty, and barriers to upward educational progress. The noticeable evidence of this can be found in the scarcity of Black PhD graduates that emerge from contexts with impoverished social conditions, which reveals the severe impact of systemic issues and the roadblocks that can keep a marginalized group of people out of higher education.

When I think of how historical racism has caused a traumatic chain reaction that creates the hindrances I describe, I see this in a visual layout, as in the chart I have created. I call this the Generational Trauma and Educational Inequity Framework. This book describes and analyzes each component of this framework and also gives a deeper understanding of educational injustice. Yet this book is also about my personal journey. It is from my heart. It mirrors the collective struggle for equity and justice for all who emerge from concrete. My hope is that you will have the heart, time, and courage to travel with me through some painful and hopeful stories from my life in the 1980s and 1990s; and that you will use my pain and hope as a lens and a plea to advocate for more resources, support, and community for those who wish to obtain a higher education—even a doctoral education—but have no means or support to do so. I deeply hope, too, that you will be inspired to persevere in seeking higher education yourself, if that is your dream.

When I was eighteen years old and sleeping in my car after a family disagreement, I prayed to God to help me overcome poverty—in all its forms: spiritual, emotional, social, and material. I prayed for help to heal and find a way to achieve a doctorate one day, which was one of my dreams. I knew that if God ever allowed me to overcome my circumstances, I would want God to use my story and do community work. That is what I have done. In 2013, I cofounded Love Beyond Walls, a nonprofit organization in Atlanta that supports those who are unhoused and impoverished, with my wife, Cecilia Lester. The organization serves the voices that are silenced and never make it to the academy: those still fighting their way through poverty, who do not have tangible examples of what is possible in the face of adversity; those experiencing homelessness while in school; those children who are facing trauma, causing them to disconnect from their lessons;

those who are growing up in communities like the ones I grew up in; those without a community of support or many positive role models; those families struggling with scarcity; and those single mothers and fathers hoping their children steer clear of trouble.

The words you will encounter here are about how I found the strength to become Tupac's rose. It is an honest reflection of how the divine grace of God, coupled with the compassion of others—some who were not my family but became my support system—provided the nurturing I needed along the way to overcome my trauma and challenges. It was God's grace, along with resilience, that brought me to where I am today. I pray that my voice is used to bring attention to what we need to do to ensure that others born in similar conditions, and against such odds, can achieve the same.

ONE

THE INCIDENT

Certain childhood memories inform your life forever. For me, it was one of the first times I realized that I was a Black boy. It was 1991, and I was nine years old. I had woken up early on a Monday morning to get myself ready for school. I did the normal things elementary school kids do when they really don't want to go to school, such as taking a long time in the bathroom and walking around the house aimlessly, hoping that somehow, miraculously, the weekend had extended itself into Monday morning. But this morning took a different turn. I overheard my mother, Connie, speaking on the phone with one of her friends in a tone filled with fear. The image of her fingers tightly gripping the long cord of our house phone and nervously shaking it until it swung rapidly is etched in my memory. It seemed she was using the motion of the cord to cope with the distressing news she was receiving.

"They did what to him?" she said.

Shortly afterward, she rushed into the only room in our house that had a television set and turned on the news. I stood by to hear more, but from her tone of voice, I knew it wasn't good. My mother turned on the television, and I immediately heard the commentators saying a name I'd never heard before: Rodney King. A few minutes later, I made my way into the room, and there were images of King being beaten by Los Angeles police officers: thirty-three blows and seven kicks. King's injuries included fractured bones, a broken right ankle, and numerous lacerations.

It was tough for me as a child to process what I was seeing. You can imagine that my mind was overwhelmed with curiosity, asking, "Why is this happening?" I came a bit farther into the room and continued to listen.

I was paralyzed with fear as she spoke on the phone about Rodney King and his unjust beating by police officers. She said, "I don't know why they do us like that." Those words were singed onto my mind. Although I didn't fully understand the extent of what was being said, I knew she must have meant that these things happen to Black people. And even though I was hearing about this event by eavesdropping, my nine-year-old brain could tell from my mom's voice that something was wrong, something beyond the usual talks she'd give me for getting dressed late or walking aimlessly around the house.

It was at that moment that I realized, for the first time in my life, that the color of my skin mattered and might bring about a different set of experiences in this world. I knew that not only would I be late to school but that this day would also remain with me for the rest of my life.

INTERNALIZING THE RODNEY KING INCIDENT

When I was five, my mother had separated from my father, Tyrone. She was now a single parent to my sister, Ashley, and me.

On the day of the Rodney King incident, the ride to school felt different, as if I were carrying something heavy inside me—both the trauma from my family's separation and the fear from realizing that something was different for me because I was a Black child. It was as if my mom's tense, frightened words that morning had cast a cloud over the rest of my day. Now, I was being hit with the reality that I am a Black child growing up during a time when Black people were being targeted as a reaction to the civil rights movement. I knew this because my mother had spoken with me about growing up as a Black boy in a world still littered with racism. I couldn't shake the feeling that I'd crossed some invisible line into a new understanding of my world.

Looking back, it was the same world that six-year-old Ruby Bridges had experienced twenty years prior when she was escorted by federal agents and the army into William Frantz Elementary School in New Orleans after the *Brown v. Board of Education* decision—which was a long-fought battle against educational injustice. A protester standing outside the school had held a sign that read, "All I want for Christmas is a clean white school."[1] It was a different time from Ruby's, but I now carried an emotional burden of not only wondering why I had to move from place to place because my family broke up but also knowing something was different in our community. Each day going to school was more than just heavy; it was a reality check to the differences that set my life, experiences, neighborhood, and school apart from others—even going to an all-Black school because of the conversations I had with my mother. I had no clue that I was inheriting what I describe in the Generational Trauma and Educational Inequity Framework as a world littered with the stains of trauma and oppressive social conditions experienced over generations.

It was the same trauma that caused the elders in my life—my grandmothers, grandfathers, and other guiding adults—to sometimes shamefully echo the sentiment, "Being Black is hard in this country because of everything we have had to overcome and are still striving to overcome." Their words, steeped in the wisdom of lived experiences, painted a vivid picture of resilience amid trauma, mistreatment, poverty, and adversity. They shed light on the ongoing journey of overcoming that defines so much of the Black experience in America—one where each generation has had to deal with the residue of what hatred and oppression caused.

When I mention racial identity, I am talking about two parts that the National Museum of African American History and Culture mentions: one externally communicated through how you are perceived, the other an internalization of how you perceive yourself.[2] When the externally imposed racial identity loudly communicates a narrative that you are perceived a certain way because of the color of your skin, this can have a severe impact on your internal beliefs, which contributes to emotional and psychological trauma. During our morning commutes, I often found myself staring out of the window, pondering how being Black was frequently associated with being wrong or mistreated in the world.

THE GRADIES

I was born a "Grady Baby," at the Grady Hospital in Atlanta.[3] Being a Grady Baby implied much more than just being born in that particular location. It reflected the reality of growing up in a city with deep, seemingly impassable economic divides.

Grady plays a critical role in the community in which I grew up. It has long been the go-to medical facility for those without access to insurance or health care options, constituting a crucial part of Atlanta's health care landscape but also, ironically, a reflection of the systemic poverty experienced by Black Atlantans. The history of Grady Memorial Hospital exemplifies this, with its origins rooted in racial segregation. Established in 1892 and named after journalist Henry W. Grady, who advocated for white supremacy post–Civil War in the form of public policy that discriminated against Black people, the hospital initially provided segregated and unequal services to Black and White patients in what was historically a Black community.[4]

The term "the Gradies" emerged from these segregated practices. Virtually every aspect of care at Grady continued to be segregated by race until the mid-twentieth century. The opening of the "New Grady" in 1958 further solidified this legacy, with segregated wings for patients.[5] However, by the 1960s, civil rights activists, including the Atlanta Student Movement and Dr. Martin Luther King Jr., led protests that prompted judicial and legislative actions to integrate medical boards and public hospitals. Grady's desegregation was officially marked by a memo from hospital superintendent Bill Pinkston on June 1, 1965, stating that all operations would be non-racial from that day forward.[6]

I was born in this hospital in 1982. It had been seventeen years since it was desegregated, yet the 1980s in Atlanta were still burdened with tension heightened by racial discrimination and deep social inequities. The city was growing and changing, but not all changes were for the better. The Atlanta Child Murders spanning from 1979 to 1981 cast a grim shadow over the city, instilling pain, fear, and uncertainty within its communities because children were the victims during the height of racial tension that lingered from the past. As the number of victims—primarily Black children and young adults—continued to rise, Atlanta was gripped by these murders of innocent children. The heartless and heinous crime not only robbed families of their loved ones but also shattered the idea of safety and security even more in the Black community.

Simultaneously, the emergence of the crack epidemic further compounded the challenges faced by the Black community in Atlanta.[7] The proliferation of crack cocaine often deeply affected whole neighborhoods, ravaged families, and fueled generations of addiction, violence, and despair in Atlanta and around the country. These twin crises, the child murders and the crack epidemic, along with racial injustice and poverty, hovered over the city alongside its national and global contributions and progress.

While Atlanta experienced economic growth and cultural vibrancy under the leadership of Maynard Holbrook Jackson Jr., the city's first Black mayor (in office 1974–1982 and 1990–1994), the pervasive influence of racial and economic injustice cast a dark cloud over progress. Even post–civil rights, systemic inequality persisted. Jackson, a trailblazer and attorney, became one of Atlanta's foremost political leaders addressing these issues and was a central leader in helping the city understand the urgent need for collective action to tackle the root causes of injustice, while helping to ensure that equal access and affirmative action were upheld for Black Atlantans, who had been left out of economic growth owing to past public policies.[8] According to Ronald Baylor, "The Atlanta of the 1970s and 1980s, still struggling with the problems created by earlier often race-based policy decisions, was very much a product of a past that had emphasized race."[9]

CAMPBELLTON ROAD

One such "race-based policy decision that had emphasized race" affected literally every moment of my life as a child—it drew the roads and boundaries that marked out the neighborhood where I grew up. When my sister and I were children, we lived with our parents in a small brick house situated off Tell Road. Tell Road intersects with Fairburn Road, a crucial connector route leading to Campbellton Road. This single road serves as a vital link connecting numerous neighborhoods and giving rise to a distinctive, tightly knit community.

Racial and geographical division was common in Atlanta. The Atlanta History Center does a great job detailing not only the flourishing of the city but also its dark past that has been littered with white supremacy. In fact, within the city limits, various streets have two different names because White residents didn't want to live on the same street as Black residents: Moreland Avenue and Briarcliff Road, Boulevard and Monroe Drive, Parkway and Charles Allen Drives, and Central Park Place and Argonne

Avenue.[10] Campbellton Road was a microcosm of a larger story not just in the city of Atlanta but in every major US city that was heavily populated with communities of Black people.[11]

During the 1980s, Campbellton Road was one of Atlanta's most economically challenged communities. Poverty created barriers for Black families and perpetuated a cycle of social inequality. In 1980, 32.5 percent of the nation's Black population lived below the poverty line, compared to 25.7 percent of Hispanic people and 10.2 percent of White people.[12] The history of Campbellton Road isn't great either, reflecting a similar trend of economic hardship and systemic neglect. Originally Cherokee land, it was later used by Confederate soldiers as a connecting point to Atlanta. Campbellton is a former settlement named for Col. Duncan Campbell, and it was the focus of Campbell County, founded in 1828.[13] The colonel was known for negotiating the 1825 treaty in which the Creek Indians ceded their land in Georgia and Alabama. This treaty was later deemed fraudulent, and the 1826 Second Treaty of Washington also ended with the Creeks ceding their land in Georgia.[14]

Campbellton Road became concentrated with Black families due to the racial divide in the city of Atlanta. The implementation of segregation laws and discriminatory housing policies forced Black families into specific neighborhoods. These communities, like mine, were often overlooked. One of the reasons I know this historical discrimination lingered and had a social and environmental effect is because I lived there. I had friends whose parents would often talk about the Black struggle in front of us. I vividly remember one friend's mother talking to another parent after football practice, saying, "It's hard being Black because to be Black is almost guaranteed that you are poor. . . ." This statement has stuck with me since I was nearly ten years old. Similar to many American cities from the 1970s through the 1990s, Atlanta was predominantly populated by Black families who struggled with poverty.[15]

I remember my neighborhood, with its dilapidated buildings; the drugs on street corners being sold; peers who, like me, were raised in single-parent households; and targeted policing with the Red Dog unit, a group known for police brutality against oppressed groups.[16] Crime didn't seem out of the ordinary. It was simply the backdrop to my daily life and the world that I inherited. The absence of healthy food options because of the food deserts and the lack of thriving local businesses were common in my neighborhood and accepted as normal because we did not know anything else outside of the economic divestment.[17] This normalization of poverty and the acceptance of these wealth gaps as "just the way things are" speaks volumes about the insidious, enduring nature of systemic racism. There were times when I could tell that these issues deeply affected the pulse of the community because that is what scarcity does: it erodes anything in its path. And with this erosion, it was very easy for people to internalize these conditions.

The struggle in Black lives was reflected in the hip-hop music of the time, with artists like Tupac, Public Enemy, Kool Moe Dee, Queen Latifah, N.W.A, and A Tribe Called Quest using music to express the realities of Black lives. Grandmaster Flash and the Furious Five's well-known songs depicted the horrid conditions of that time. One song, "The Message," captures the raw essence of life in Black neighborhoods during the 1980s and speaks to the social living conditions that made the context of violence, drugs, and oppression visibly real and raw.[18] The song's imagery of "Broken glass everywhere / People pissing on the stairs, you know they just don't care" doesn't just sketch a scene; it screams of the abandonment and decay these neighborhoods endured, ignored by those who designed Black communities to be this way.

When the lyrics go further—"Got no money to move out, I guess, I got no choice"—they speak to the entrapment of poverty and the feeling of being stuck with no way out. When the song mentions "Rats in the front room, roaches in the back," it's not just talking about rodents but the pervasive, inescapable conditions that many were forced to call home. The cycle of poverty and crime is painted in their music with mentions of "Junkies in the alley with a baseball bat" and a man's car being repossessed, a narrative too familiar in communities constantly under siege by drugs, facing the rise of the crack and heroin epidemic, and the crushing weight of financial despair. Finally, the phrase "Don't push me / cause I'm close to the edge" captures how much struggle there was, how people could be on the brink of desperation, and how much emotional weight it takes to navigate these conditions. These lyrics capture what it meant to be Black in America and the fine line between surviving and breaking down.

In *Between the World and Me,* Ta-Nehisi Coates writes of growing up in Baltimore, "To be Black in the Baltimore of my youth was to be naked before the elements of the world, before all the guns, fists, knives, crack, rape, and disease. The nakedness is not an error, nor pathology. The nakedness is the correct and intended result of policy, the predictable upshot of people forced for centuries to live under fear."[19] Replace the word *Baltimore* with *Atlanta*, and you have an accurate description of my childhood. I was indeed "naked before the elements of the world." And I would add, "naked in a world that I had inherited." From my earliest days in Atlanta to my current reflections on its significance, one thing remains clear: the lessons learned and challenges faced in this city have far-reaching implications for our understanding of social justice and equity in America.

FROM ATLANTA TO THE NATION

Growing up, I was exposed to the widespread injustice that many Black communities across the nation faced during that time and still face to this day. In this environment, marked by poverty, I witnessed firsthand how families suffered, trauma unfolded, and scarcity caused real harm to my family and my peers as we all attempted to navigate the world we had inherited.

These challenges were not unique to Atlanta. Similar community challenges were evident in Baltimore, Los Angeles, Oakland, Detroit, Chicago, and other cities where pervasive poverty and limited upward economic mobility create structural roadblocks to social, personal, and educational pursuits. This was especially true for those of us who aspired to break free but lacked the necessary support and connections. As a child, grappling with these complex realities that were largely out of my control was overwhelming. Hearing adults discuss scarce resources, underfunded schools, overcrowded classrooms, and low college attendance rates among Black people made it difficult to dream of a future beyond my immediate surroundings. In many ways, it felt like what my friends and I would call "the trap."[20]

Every day, as my mom drove us to school, I couldn't help but notice how our family wasn't together. I was always acutely aware of our family separation and struggle. Witnessing my mother juggle multiple jobs caused me to be aware of how hard she was working to keep up with everything and how that meant that she would have to devote a lot of her time to work. This, coupled with the social climate, made me realize my own racial identity at a very young age—and made me realize that to be Black meant that you had to journey through a different set of social rules, which often meant that you were doing all you could to survive while navigating a world that viewed you as a social threat.

It was hard to understand the world that I was inheriting and what that meant for me in every social environment I was exposed to, whether it was the community, school, church (the times I went with my mother), or other environments. I began to understand, though, that the environment around me seemed set in place to stifle dreams, bar the pathway to academic achievement, and make it harder for a child to have any aspirations beyond surroundings that contained these types of social conditions. This impacted and affected my self-esteem and confidence, making it challenging to envision a future where I could succeed or be anything more than what I saw in my environment. Emotionally, I felt a sense of hopelessness and frustration in my understanding of the world at such a young age.

POST TRAUMATIC SLAVE SYNDROME

While numerous historical texts outline the broad strokes of racism's timeline in America, spanning from the arrival of the first enslaved Africans through the bloodshed of the Civil War into Reconstruction and across the pivotal civil rights movement, these texts—frequently written by White scholars—often paint a picture of closure, as if the deep-seated injustices of bygone eras had been conclusively addressed and relegated to history.[21] The pervasiveness of this whitewashing of history obscures the impact of what Dr. Joy DeGruy calls *post traumatic slave syndrome* and does little to advance understanding of the phenomena detailed in the framework I created to understand the educational and other challenges seen in urban centers.

DeGruy, an academic researcher, lecturer, and former professor of social work, writes powerfully on how trauma can be passed down generationally. She makes a fascinating connection between historical suffering and the transgenerational trauma that we see in the collective trauma experienced by Black people. She writes:

> Contemporary social scientists might offer an explanation as to why an African American boy might feel disrespected

by a peer that simply looks at him. They may suggest that television, newspapers and magazines projecting negative images of black males as pitiable, ignorant, violent and criminal have contributed to the overall poor self-images of black boys. Black scholars might even point out that music videos and movies depicting masculine and feminine beauty neatly wrapped in fine white features and straight hair have further deteriorated the self images of black boys and girls, causing them to despise the reflection in the mirror. And they would be right. However, what is not often addressed is the role our history has played in producing these negative perceptions, images and behaviors. We rarely look to our history to understand how African Americans adapted their behavior over centuries in order to survive the stifling effects of chattel slavery, effects which are evident today. I believe that the behaviors in the scenarios described above, as well as many others, are in large part related to trans-generational adaptations associated with the past traumas of slavery and on-going oppression. I have termed this condition "Post Traumatic Slave Syndrome," or PTSS.[22]

Her work is brilliant in that she helps us to see that trauma can be experienced trans-generationally, when safe spaces have not been created to keep up with the layered effects of trauma or have not been cared for both personally and collectively at a mass scale. She makes a case that just because we see some people acquire fame, status, or success, the historical trauma born of oppression—in the form of systemic abuse, lynching, mistreatment, and denial of access to mental health support to process and work through that trauma (among many other horrific things that explain the conditions in which we see Black communities suffer)—does not just go away.

DeGruy continues:

So what is trauma? Trauma is an injury caused by an outside, usually violent, force, event or experience. We can experience this injury physically, emotionally, psychologically, and/or spiritually. Traumas can upset our equilibrium and sense of well-being. If a trauma is severe enough it can distort our attitudes and beliefs. Such distortions often result in dysfunctional behaviors, which can in turn produce unwanted consequences. If one traumatic experience can result in distorted attitudes, dysfunctional behaviors and unwanted consequences, this pattern is magnified exponentially when a person repeatedly experiences severe trauma, and it is much worse when the traumas are caused by human beings.[23]

That morning in 1991, when I saw the video footage of Rodney King's beating at the hands of the police, was when I first recognized that collective trauma was present because of the social climate. I didn't know what the term *trauma* meant at that time or even know that word at all. All I knew was that the Rodney King incident made me start questioning everything about the color of my skin and what kind of world we lived in—a world that accepted violence toward people who looked like me and a world that caused me to join the embodied collective trauma that we experienced as Black folks. I wondered what type of world I had inherited, and what had led to the fear I heard in my mom's voice as she tried to shield my sister, Ashley, and me from a reality too harsh for our young minds.

That fear, that sense of protectiveness, is something I still carry with me now more than ever as I try to guide my own children through these same realities after witnessing Black lives being claimed, like the Central Park Five, Trayvon Martin, Michael Brown, George Floyd, Breonna Taylor, Sandra Bland, Atatiana Jefferson, Elijah McClain, Aiyana Stanley-Jones, Rekia Boyd, Korryn Gaines,

Michelle Cusseaux, Mya Hall, and others. The Rodney King incident wasn't just a news story. It was a heavy and brutal reality, a piece of a much larger puzzle tracing back to the remnants of Jim Crow laws—the harsh regulations that enforced racial segregation and stripped away the rights of Black Americans in the South from the late 1800s until the civil rights movements of the 1960s.

TRAUMA'S ORIGINS

The post–Jim Crow era inflicted severe trauma on millions of Black people, particularly those who endured it firsthand, and their children, creating lasting generational burdens. In her dissertation "Jim Crow's Legacy: Segregation Stress Syndrome," Dr. Ruth K. Thompson-Miller writes:

> The collective long-lasting psychological effects connected with the racial violence that occurred in the total institution are a critical aspect. In the interviews, African Americans shared how on a daily basis they found themselves dealing with anxiety, fear, humiliation, shame, and stress. The narratives were analyzed utilizing the extended case method. . . . [This thesis] explores symptoms of a "segregation stress syndrome" for the chronic, enduring, extremely painful experiences and responses to the total institution of Jim Crow that are indicated by numerous respondents in this research project. Preliminary findings indicate that the symptoms of "segregation stress syndrome" are similar to PTSD symptoms documented in psychiatric literature. However, "segregation stress syndrome" differs from PTSD because the traumatic experience was not a one-time occurrence; it was sustained, over time, in African American communities. In addition, the racial violence that occurred was a form of systematic chronic stress, the type that has been shown to have a detrimental impact on a person's psychological well-being.[24]

This generational trauma affects millions of Black people because research shows that trauma travels through generations. I believe we also need to trace this trauma into educational spaces and unpack how it shows up as educational injustice. In fact, the 1992 Los Angeles riots sparked by the acquittal of the officers involved in King's beating brought to the forefront issues not just of police brutality but of the enduring impact of systemic racism, from chattel slavery to the hatred that showed up in public policy, known as Jim Crow laws.[25]

I once heard my grandfather say, "They took away some laws that discriminated, but they did not take it from the hearts of those who stood by the laws." The King incident captured on video for the world to see did more than just expose the brutality of the police and the racial tension in Los Angeles. It forced White people to confront a haunting question: Why, long after Jim Crow's shadow was supposedly lifted, was violence against Black and impoverished communities still so rampant in the 1980s and 1990s? Why did the very system that once sanctioned such hatred still perpetuate violence against Black people? Why does it still do so to this day?

One of my professors once remarked that partial rights and citizenship for Black people in America didn't fully start to materialize until the 1970s. When examining an abbreviated timeline of Black history, it becomes clear what my professor meant and what Dr. DeGruy's work was trying to communicate. Since 1619—a timespan of 376 years—significant progress has been made, but my professor suggested it wasn't until Shirley Chisholm's name appeared on the ballot for president of the United States that we, as formerly enslaved Black people who had been—in US government counts determining representation in Congress—considered three-fifths of a person, truly began to claim an abbreviated version of citizenship.[26] And even then, we continued to face heightened racial tensions and discrimination.

Fast-forward, I am writing this during the second presidential term of Donald Trump, and we are witnessing a rapid erosion of constitutional protections meant to safeguard historically marginalized communities—especially Black and Brown ones. Through executive orders, DEI (Diversity, Equity, and Inclusion) initiatives have been targeted, with mandates being dismantled under the guise of eliminating "divisive concepts" and promoting "merit-based" systems and a "colorblind" society—in which color has always played a role in the way people where I am from were treated.[27]

A merit-based society is subjective and can be used to further discriminate because it relies solely on merit—but who gets to determine what constitutes merit? That determination itself is a form of power. Terms like *woke, DEI, critical race theory* (CRT), and *social justice* have become dog-whistle expressions used to target the fight for Black and Brown equity. The push for a meritocracy in a world structurally designed to disadvantage certain groups emboldens and empowers a society without guardrails, allowing exclusion to persist.

Trump's immediate presidential actions in the first few days of office have not only affected federal policies but have also influenced major corporations like Target, Meta, Walmart, and McDonald's to reduce or entirely eliminate their DEI efforts, signaling a retreat from equity-based commitments—where even the mention of the terms DEI and equity have been co-opted to somehow mean that Black and Brown people have not earned what we have achieved, and our progress has somehow been given to us unfairly. A recent meme circulating on social media claims that DEI stands for "Didn't Earn It," but Black people responded with a powerful counter message: "Definitely Earned It."

The collective trauma of these rollbacks is deeply felt by communities already struggling against systemic inequities. Adding to this harm, the Air Force recently removed the Tuskegee Airmen from its curriculum, a deliberate erasure of Black excellence and

A TIMELINE OF RACIAL OPPRESSION AND RESISTANCE
From Enslavement to Los Angeles Riots

1619—Slavery comes to North America: Enslaved Africans are brought to Jamestown, Virginia, marking the beginning of slavery in North America.

1793—Rise of the cotton industry: Eli Whitney's invention of the cotton gin revolutionized the cotton industry, increasing the demand for enslaved labor and causing more harm to be done to Africans.

1831—Nat Turner's revolt: Nat Turner leads a rebellion of enslaved people resisting the enslavement of Africans and harm to Black bodies.

1831—Abolitionism and the Underground Railroad: Abolitionists help enslaved Africans to escape through the Underground Railroad where Harriet Tubman's liberating work became central to the freedom of those oppressed.

1857—Dred Scott case: The Supreme Court's decision in Scott v. Sanford denies citizenship and constitutional rights to all Black people, adding to the continued hardship of Africans in the United States.

1861–1865—Civil War and emancipation: The Civil War led to the abolition of slavery with the Emancipation Proclamation being signed and the Thirteenth Amendment ratified, which was followed by Juneteenth for those enslaved in Galveston, Texas.

1865—The post-slavery South and Reconstruction: The period after the Civil War, known as Reconstruction, involved efforts to integrate those who had been enslaved by white supremacy into the social, political, and labor spaces of society. This, however, was met with extreme resistance and was the catalyst and foundation for the formation and launch of the Ku Klux Klan.

1896—"Separate but equal" doctrine established: Plessy v. Ferguson legitimized racial segregation through the doctrine of "separate but equal."

1900s—Rise of intellectual Black leaders: Leaders like Booker T. Washington, W. E. B. Du Bois, Ida B. Wells, Mary Church Terrell, Anna Julia Cooper, and George Washington Carver emerged, advocating for civil rights and education and speaking on behalf of the condition of Black people.

1909—Founding of the NAACP: The National Association for the Advancement of Colored People was established to fight racial discrimination and advocate for civil rights among those who were being attacked by the legal system.

1920s—Harlem Renaissance: An intellectual, social, and artistic explosion was centered in Harlem, New York City, during the 1920s. This movement celebrated Black cultural expressions and advocated for a new identity among Black people, encouraging a new racial consciousness and cultural pride.

1930s–1940s—Redlining and racial segregation in housing: The Federal Housing Administration's practice of redlining in the 1930s and 1940s institutionalized and legalized racial segregation in housing. This excluded Black people from accessing mortgages and increased the wealth gap between Black and White people.[1] This practice significantly limited a Black family's ability to own a home and build wealth for the generations that would come after them.

1940s—Exclusion and segregation of Black soldiers: Despite serving in World War II, Black soldiers faced segregation within the US military—only being viewed as less-than. Upon returning home, they were also excluded from many of the benefits provided by the GI Bill due to discrimination.

1954—Brown v. Board of Education: This Supreme Court decision declared school segregation unconstitutional, beginning the process of integration in schools, which was met with White resistance in many states.

1955—Emmett Till's murder and Montgomery Bus Boycott: The brutal murder of Emmett Till, a young Black boy who was abducted in the middle of the night while visiting family, then tortured and lynched in Mississippi in 1955 after being accused of offending a White woman, Carolyn Bryant, fueled outrage. And Rosa Parks' refusal to give up her bus seat to a White man led to the Montgomery Bus Boycott, a pivotal event in the civil rights movement.

1963—Birmingham church bombing: The bombing of the Sixteenth Street Baptist Church by White supremacists murdered four young Black

---

[1]Leonard E. Egede et al., "Modern Day Consequences of Historic Redlining: Finding a Path Forward," *Journal of General Internal Medicine* 38, no. 6 (February 6, 2023): 1534-37, www.ncbi.nlm.nih.gov/pmc/articles/PMC9901820/.

girls, which revealed the deep hatred and the violent resistance to integration and left a traumatic mark on the Black community.

1963—"I Have a Dream" speech: Martin Luther King Jr. delivered a transformative speech during the March on Washington advocating for civil and economic rights and an end to racism, which was at the core of his triple evil theory.

1964—Civil Rights Act passed: A landmark legislation outlawing discrimination based on race, color, religion, sex, or national origin was enacted under President Lyndon Johnson.

1965—Selma to Montgomery marches: These demonstrations brought thousands of Black people together to take a stand against discriminatory voting practices, leading to the passage of the Voting Rights Act of 1965.

1965—Voting Rights Act enacted: This legislative act prohibited racial discrimination in voting.

Late 1960s—Black power movement: This movement reminded Black people of their worth and heritage and advocated for racial dignity, self-reliance, equity, and equality for Black people.

1968—Assassination of Martin Luther King Jr.: MLK Jr. was assassinated at the Lorraine Motel while taking a stand against poverty in Memphis, Tennessee, alongside sanitation workers.

1968—Fair Housing Act: Law passed to ensure equal and equitable housing opportunities for Black people and making it a federal crime to discriminate based on race, creed, or national origin.

1972—Shirley Chisholm runs for president: Shirley Chisholm became the first major-party Black candidate and the first-ever woman candidate for president of the United States seven years after the Voting Rights Act was passed.

1978—Bakke decision and affirmative action: The Supreme Court upheld affirmative action but struck down racial quotas in college admissions.[2]

1982—The "War on Drugs" enacted: This year during the Reagan presidency marked the continuation of a series of policies initiated by Richard Nixon (1973) that aimed at combating drug use. These

[2]Richard A. Posner, "The Bakke Case and the Future of 'Affirmative Action,'" *California Law Review* 67 (1979): 171-89, https://chicagounbound.uchicago.edu/cgi/viewcontent.cgi?article=2812&context=journal_articles.

policies disproportionately affected the Black community, filling prisons with Black people who committed nonviolent crimes.

1983—"A Nation at Risk" published in April: The National Commission on Excellence in Education was established by Secretary of Education Terrel H. Bell in 1981. The report warned that the "educational foundations of American society had been eroded by the rising tide of mediocrity."[3] These reforms often led to more standardized testing and strict accountability measures, which ended up hurting schools in Black communities the most.[4]

1984—The Comprehensive Crime Control Act: This act established mandatory minimum sentencings for drug offenses. It greatly impacted the Black community because of the War on Drugs campaign that targeted communities of color.[5]

1986—The Anti-Drug Abuse Act of 1986: The act established an imbalance and sentencing disparity between crack and powder cocaine, disproportionately impacting Black communities because of the prevalence of crack cocaine in urban areas.

1992—Los Angeles riots: Riots in Los Angeles reflected ongoing racial tensions following the acquittal of police officers charged in the beating of Rodney King.[6]

---

[3]Anya Kamenetz, "What 'A Nation at Risk' Got Wrong, and Right, About U.S. Schools," *NPR*, April 29, 2018, www.npr.org/sections/ed/2018/04/29/604986823 /what-a-nation-at-risk-got-wrong-and-right-about-u-s-schools.

[4]Valerie Strauss, "The Landmark 'A Nation at Risk' Called for Education Reform 35 Years Ago. Here's How It Was Bungled," *The Washington Post*, April 26, 2018, www.washingtonpost.com/news/answer-sheet/wp/2018/04/26/the-land mark-a-nation-at-risk-called-for-education-reform-35-years-ago-heres-how-it -was-bungled.

[5]Ranya Shannon, "3 Ways the 1994 Crime Bill Continues to Hurt Communities of Color," *Center for American Progress*, May 10, 2019, www.americanprogress.org /article/3-ways-1994-crime-bill-continues-hurt-communities-color.

[6]Condensed from "Black History Milestones: Timeline," History.com, October 14, 2009, updated January 24, 2024, www.history.com/topics/black-history/black -history-milestones. While not comprehensive, this timeline provides insight into the enduring struggle through the 1970s, 1980s, and 1990s for Black people, offering a backdrop to better understand the educational challenges I'll explore rooted in poverty and trauma. I added additional events not included in the History.com timeline.

resilience in the face of institutional racism. And later they had to add it back when backlash began forming against the unjust removal of this important history.[28] These actions represent a troubling regression, illustrating how the fragile progress made in recent decades is being unraveled, leaving us to wrestle with the lingering question of how personhood, equity, and justice will survive under such a political assault.

Consider the abbreviated timeline, which doesn't even do justice to the atrocities that were experienced.

The hardships endured by the Black community, such as poverty, housing discrimination, and educational resource scarcity, are a direct connection to the hardships of the past and help us to understand the linkage between generational and educational disparities that we see in urban centers.

Long before I had any real knowledge about Black history and struggle, I would often ask my teachers at my school, Mary McCloud Bethune Elementary and Chapel Hill Elementary, why Black people had to suffer like Rodney King. Unfortunately, we weren't learning much about Black history in school. While my teachers would occasionally, briefly point toward Black people who broke through the oppression, these lessons were not in-depth enough to help my young mind understand why oppression needed to be broken through. Despite the teachers' efforts to identify people who had overcome the injustices of racism, I still felt like something was off—I couldn't fully grasp the weight of history. And while I believe educators shielded me and my peers from the full truth, it ultimately contributed to burying history and keeping me unaware. All I knew was that those barriers were established long before I arrived.

And furthermore, if this was the landscape that I had to navigate, what about the other Black or Brown children who, like me, were born into poverty in the 1980s and stepped into a world already steeped in such deep-seated challenges? My childhood, sprinkled with dreams and innocence, was also shadowed by a cloud of history that contained systemic injustice, trauma, terror, and fear. Every blow Rodney King took felt like a collective blow to the Black community, each reminding those who watched about the mountains and hurdles we were still facing simply because of the color of our skin. As a child immersed in poverty, the full weight and complexity of this history journeyed with me every single day as I attempted to break the chains of systemic injustice and not get caught up in the cycle of the New Jim Crow.[29]

A MOMENT OF REFLECTION

Reflect on your experiences. If you are Black: Have you fully processed history in a way that has allowed you to heal from the discrimination, poverty, or other systemic challenges you may have faced as a result of this history? How has this impacted your life? Have you ever felt the weight of these barriers within your community or the one you emerged from? Did you grow up in blighted neighborhoods where urban hassles were present or part of the social landscape? To have lived during this time was to know firsthand what it meant to be Black after Jim Crow and civil rights, but it was also a time of great pride in being Black. Despite generational trauma, discrimination, and systemic barriers, it is possible to rise to your full potential.

If you're not Black: Consider the many barriers discussed in this chapter that you may have been unaware of—barriers that exist right from the start and keep those experiencing them from feeling they could achieve their personal or educational dreams. How does this new understanding change your perspective? How can this knowledge help you better understand and support those who face these challenges?

Engaging with these questions can lead to a deeper awareness and a shift in perspective, starting a journey of healing, or helping to create a more equitable society. All of these reflections can help prepare you for the lenses that you are about to put on.

TWO

THE FEAR OF A BLACK CHILD

I didn't know what the fight was about. All I know is that it was loud and that it started with screams, then shattering glass. I hid in my room. I was five years old and, to this day, I can feel the anxiety I felt then.

I heard my mom scream in fear as she tried to escape my father's violent rage. "Terence, we need to go!" she shouted. Immediately, she scooped up Ashley, then just one year old, and threw a jacket on me. Then we were all out the front door in seconds. Forever.

Escaping the violence, we walked a little over a mile to my mom's aunt's home. My mom was out of breath, and this picture in my mind lets me know that fear and anxiety had overcome her. I didn't understand why I had been taken on this long, unexpected walk. All I knew was that I was moving farther away from the only home I knew.

When you're that young, it's tough for your mind to process traumatic, life-defining moments like this, especially those filled with rage, shock, and anxiety. It was even more traumatic to witness my mother facing these emotions too, collectively experiencing the same fear and uncertainty.

I will never forget the fear I felt. But I will also never forget where it all took place. I can distinctly remember the smells, the floor plan, the brick, the cabinets, the carpet, my room, and right where that fear was born. Built in the 1950s, our house evoked memories of old seventies decor with an earth-tone carpet, brightly colored tiles in the bathrooms, and wood paneling. I'll never forget the fresh scent of the wallpaper or the look of the cream-colored kitchen countertops. I can still remember overhearing my grandmother and mother talking about how the first five years of my life, when my sister and I had both parents in the home, were littered with violence, poverty, and emotional abuse. It had all led up to my mother's decision to remove herself, and us, from that environment and make a fresh start.

This episode marked the beginning of my chronic anxiety. At least, that is what I told my therapist who asked me when I first felt afraid from trauma, when I found the courage to start therapy in my twenties. All I knew was that one minute I was playing with those green army action figures that kids got for Christmas in the 1980s, and the next minute I was out on the street with my mom and my little sister, screams echoing in the background while we all walked away from home.

Violence is horrific because it can shatter and disrupt the concept of home, especially when the idea of home is supposed to be one of safety. As a young boy, this reality was overwhelming and terrifying. Hearing my elders talk about how Black people were treated poorly and misrepresented on television in the eighties and nineties added to the trauma of family dysfunction. It can create memories that haunt you in your sleep and linger in the back of your mind. Even today, the memories of those times haunt me, reminding me of the long road I had to travel to heal and work through those emotions.

I still shed uncontrollable tears when I recall that day when my mom, my sister, and I left our home. Emotions run deep, and the trauma from those moments runs deeper. And even though my father and I were able to reconcile, repair, forgive, and forge a deep friendship toward the end of his life, I chose to tell this part of the story not to shame him or trigger anyone but to explain the entirety of my journey of trauma and its relationship to my early educational challenges, poverty, and injustice.

Home should have been a place where I found safety, nurturing, and a sense of belonging. Home should have empowered me and set me up for success in the world, despite the cards already stacked against me. And yet, amid the violence and chaos of my childhood home environment, I began to lose my concept of home. Domestic violence traumatizes everyone involved—those who experience it and those who hear and see it happen. It is the type of trauma that affects your relationships and informs how you feel about yourself, and it can determine the life choices you make—choices in your teens, twenties, thirties, forties, fifties, sixties, or as long as you can remember the pain.

If there were one dominant emotion I experienced that morning when my mother walked away from our home with me and my sister, it was fear: fear of the unknown, fear of seeing my brave mom in tears, fear of what we were going to do next. These are memories I still carry in my heart, mind, and soul from growing up on Campbellton Road. I just remember the fear.

A ONE-PARENT HOME

My mother was now a single parent. This wasn't easy, especially after long, tiring days of having to do everything herself. She juggled multiple jobs and did the best she could, enduring and overcoming challenges that seemed insurmountable. It took my mom a few years to regain stability. Eventually, she bought a home less than two miles away from our previous residence on Tell Road.

However, while my mother eventually found stability in housing, I did not find it emotionally because I was still dealing with the trauma of violence and anxiety, and I am pretty sure that the effect of this lingered in her too. It was probably hard for me to find stability emotionally because before we were able to secure our own place, we moved around a few times. We lived a brief transient life because my mother was trying to do everything she could to provide for two children while dealing with the trauma that came along with what she had faced with my father and just trying to survive. For some time, we relied on the generosity of family members and moved from one relative's house to another until my mother leveraged her resilience to become stable on her own.

My mother worked part-time as a custodian in the evenings and on the weekends, cleaning buildings outside her regular job as a cafeteria manager in schools, all while striving to continue her education at a time when online classes weren't an option. She juggled taking me to her second job and her own classes. All this while managing a household with two children on a salary of less than $18,000 a year, sometimes without the convenience of a car. She eventually went back to school to complete two master's degrees and, later in life, an educational doctorate in clinical counseling. She always showed an inner strength, a resilience in Black women that often stems from a history of overcoming myriad injustices.

Watching my mother and grandmother Gloria, I believe this inner strength comes from a deep sense of community, their faith in God, and an unwavering belief in their own worth despite the history of hardships our ancestors faced. Black women have often had to display this level of courage and resilience while, in many ways, their strength and dignity have not always been affirmed. It saddens me that Black women still find themselves in the present moment having to remain resilient, fight for their worth, and demand to be heard and acknowledged. This is especially disheartening when they have given so much of themselves and carried generations with their unparalleled strength. While addressing a group of Black people in California about the plight of the Black woman, Malcolm X once said, "The most disrespected person in America is the Black woman. The most unprotected person in America is the Black woman. The most neglected person in America is the Black woman."[1] Reflecting on this, I am reminded of the many Black women who daily find themselves in just this situation: navigating deep societal barriers and holding together families while dealing with deep trauma in their own and their families' lives—and doing so largely on their own.

"WHAT IT WAS REALLY ABOUT"

I didn't learn until much later that the shattering of my home life had played out against the backdrop of an era that was already unfavorable to Black people in the South. Scholars have demonstrated an inescapable link between deprived social living conditions—that is, poverty—and family violence.[2] The strain of the lack of resources, social pressures, economic hardships, limited opportunities, and injustices can lead to increased tension and frustration within not just households but whole communities. Poverty coupled with systemic injustice can cause a never-ending cycle of violence and frustration, which ultimately can impact children and who they become in society. These types of social and emotional challenges can create high levels of tension, raise levels of stress, and add deeper burdens and conflict within a family or community. In turn, these very circumstances increase the probability of domestic violence, thus creating a cycle of trauma.[3]

These inherently vicious cycles were exacerbated in the 1980s under the Reagan administration, when social stigma against Black people seemed to escalate dramatically. This was due in part to the War on Drugs and the crack epidemic, with its systemic mass incarceration and racial disparities and injustices. Instigated by the

Nixon administration, the War on Drugs saw the numbers of incarcerated rise from three hundred thousand to over two million people. Of those two million, two-thirds were people of color.[4] This is important because, post–Jim Crow and the civil rights movement, racial discrimination increased through public policy and rhetoric that framed Black people, already suffering from poverty, as criminals. John Ehrlichman, a Nixon aide and Watergate co-conspirator, confirmed that the War on Drugs was aimed at disrupting Black communities.[5] Dan Baum interviewed Ehrlichman and captured his words about how this policy was intentionally designed:

"You want to know what this was really all about?" he asked with the bluntness of a man who, after public disgrace and a stretch in federal prison, had little left to protect. "The Nixon campaign in 1968, and the Nixon White House after that, had two enemies: the antiwar left and Black people. . . . We knew we couldn't make it illegal to be either against the war or Black, but by getting the public to associate the hippies with marijuana and Blacks with heroin, and then criminalizing both heavily, we could disrupt those communities. We could arrest their leaders, raid their homes, break up their meetings, and vilify them night after night on the evening news. Did we know we were lying about the drugs? Of course we did."[6]

By the time Reagan took office, the War on Drugs had escalated into a strategy that disproportionately impacted communities of color, socially framing Black people as undeserving and using political rhetoric and power to embed this into the social fabric. In her 2010 discourses, Michelle Alexander compellingly articulated that the War on Drugs evolved into a modern iteration of Jim Crow, explicitly targeting racial minorities.[7]

The 1980s revealed the persistent racial discrimination within United States economic and social policies. The period's economic reforms, characterized by tax cuts for the wealthy and reduced social welfare spending, disproportionately harmed Black and Brown communities, exacerbating income inequality and reducing access to essential services. Donovan X. Ramsey's *When Crack Was King* helped to shed light on the personal narratives from this time period, emphasizing the deep impact of governmental policies on Black communities during the crack epidemic.[8] The period's rhetoric included references to "welfare queens," further perpetuating stereotypes that Black people and Black women were lazy and solely sought to benefit from government assistance, without addressing the reality that many Black people lived in impoverished neighborhoods and relied on subsidies to survive from day to day.[9] Additionally, such policies failed to acknowledge how political power dynamics hindered poverty alleviation efforts.

That is why Dr. Martin Luther King Jr. constantly spoke about "the other America." In this other America, while some communities flourished, a vast number of Black people faced the daily struggles of unemployment, substandard living conditions, insurmountable systemic barriers, and the persistent inequalities that needed urgent attention. If you notice in the historical timeline, Black people didn't have equal access to housing until 1968, which carried over into the seventies, eighties, and nineties through lingering redlining practices. Even today we can travel to cities that are populated with Black and Brown communities and still see the effects of these harmful practices.

Many times, when people quote Dr. Martin Luther King Jr.'s speech, commonly labeled the "I Have a Dream" speech, they focus on the parts that inspired millions to march on Washington. However, King's speech also spoke to the harsh realities of racial injustice:

But one hundred years later, the Negro still is not free. One hundred years later, the life of the Negro is still sadly crippled by the manacles of segregation and the chains of discrimination. One hundred years later, the Negro lives on a lonely island of poverty in the midst of a vast ocean of material prosperity. One hundred years later, the Negro is still languishing in the corners of American society and finds himself in exile in his own land. And so we've come here today to dramatize a shameful condition. In a sense, we've come to our nation's capital to cash a check.[10]

ABUSE AT SCHOOL

Witnessing and experiencing such violence and deprivation at a young age impacted my development and understanding of both my world and my place in it. It certainly very deeply impacted my experience in the classroom, and I experienced many challenges at school. I remember being afraid—afraid to use my voice, share my feelings and opinions, even engage with the lessons. There were times I felt deeply afraid to be around people.

I did not ask to grow up in a world that I was afraid to be in. It just happened. It made me angry, and that showed up in the way I began processing information. I often felt disconnected from the lessons, remained quiet in class, experienced emotional distress that led me to not be unable to answer questions when teachers called on me. My voice felt frozen.

Instead of receiving empathy or support from teachers, I was met with punishment. One teacher decided to lock me in a closet in a school I was attending called Florence Jackson Academy off Fairburn Road (less than a mile away from Campbellton Road) as a disciplinary action because she asked me a question in front of other students that I would not answer. I was in elementary school and still remember all the children laughing at me when she placed me in that closet, which added to my trauma. Little did she know that she was retraumatizing me all over again. Florence Jackson Academy, while seen as a pillar in the community for Black children, was a private school that practiced corporal punishment, which is the use of physical force to discipline students. This meant that the principal and other school leaders would use a belt to whip and punish children for misbehaving or getting into trouble. I remember times when I was whipped multiple times, and it was terrifying—an experience that still sends deep chills through me today. It was a fear I will never forget. Although the school tried its best to uplift Black children in a world perpetuating social bruising tied to injustice, it marked the beginning of my fear of school and my experience of educational injustice—aggravated by the indirect injustice from the larger social context. My educational experience was thus deeply compounded with the generational trauma carried by Black people due to white supremacy.

I couldn't believe it. I specifically remember thinking about the arguing and yelling the night before between my parents when my teacher walked around the class asking for students to participate in the discussion. When she called on me, I didn't say anything, which appeared to upset her and was followed by this extreme punishment. This further complicated my idea of home and made my pain more real both at home and in school, causing me to feel overwhelmed and even more disconnected from lessons—which was a form of educational injustice. As I reflect on these experiences today, I feel deep emotions about growing up during a time when segregated schools still existed—not by law but through city designs that concentrated Black communities based on income, highways, roads, and access. This environment led educators in my context to believe they needed to be harder on Black children to prepare them for a world filled with racism and discrimination. Even now, writing this brings tears to my eyes.

THE IMPACT OF TRAUMA ON EDUCATION

I've worked through much of my own pain and trauma to even understand all the inequities that were barriers to the educational goals in my life. The lack of stability in my home, as well as the social conditions and systemic factors of the time, profoundly contributed to my struggles in school. This, in turn, caused me to be ill-prepared for academics and affected how I felt around people. I was afraid—afraid of communicating with others because the violence itself caused me to withdraw—and unable to focus. This was not because I didn't have the intellect for it but because it was hard to focus with trauma in the way. I question how you can truly be stable in school when you feel emotionally unstable at home and in the world around you.

Research shows that when children are exposed to violence, it disrupts feelings of safety and security and can cause fear to constantly be in the back of their minds. Researchers have examined how domestic violence exacerbates trauma, potentially leading to PTSD and a loss of trust in those around them.[11] This research explains how such violence shows up cognitively. It can impede a child's behavioral development, harm their emotional capacity to understand, and cause a disconnected experience in school settings.[12] Also, trauma is not only violence based but consists of anything that can impact the emotional well-being of a child.

This understanding reveals an additional layer and potential barrier for Black children and children of color who face societal and racial injustices that create these "stressors."[13] Trauma is often rooted in disruptions to a sense of safety and security, either within the home or societally, and these disruptions instill fear and uncertainty. This can carry over into social or academic experiences and are exacerbated by pressures stemming from systemic injustice.[14] As DeGruy illustrates, from a collective trauma perspective, the trauma from injustices committed against Africans brought to the United States has had a lingering psychological effect on their descendants.[15] This trauma permeates everyday life for Black people in the United States today and reveals the enduring impact of white supremacy and social harm.

By considering DeGruy's analysis alongside the social conditions that perpetuate trauma in both home and community, the connection between personal and transgenerational trauma—the latter referring to how traumatic experiences and their effects can be passed from one generation to the next, often subconsciously—becomes a lens to understand the enormity of trauma in children, especially those who are students.[16] That was my experience in school, and I am sure many others can both relate to dealing with this unique type of trauma that stems from a child's home environment and understand how this is compounded by a long history of trauma. If I know one thing to be true, it is the difficulty of navigating the extreme external and internal pressures to reach any type of academic height. The realities of urban life, with its normalization of poverty and systemic racism and violence, create an environment where trauma thrives and can be passed down from generation to generation. This trauma, combined with the personal toll it takes on the minds of children, teens, and young adults, sets up barriers even before a child comes of age. Overcoming these barriers can knock people out long before they can reach their potential. I believe that educational challenges are connected to history, and the trauma from that history can affect social living conditions, which in turns creates the environment of educational injustice. In fact, generational, environmental, emotional, and social trauma can all impact the educational paths of children born into a world of injustices.

THE URGENCY OF TRAUMA-INFORMED CARE

My mind often reflects back to my five-year-old self and the day my family life fell apart. I find myself wondering what might have been if things had been different, healthier, and in a society that did not create such conditions for Black families to navigate—a world seemingly set up for the destruction of communities and human potential. While exploring trauma in this chapter, it's crucial to understand the weight, hardship, struggles, and obstacles placed in a community and a person's life both socially and personally as they journey through school. We must truly understand the trauma a person has to navigate to overcome their struggles—which is not easy when coming from an environment that seems designed for their structural failure, all while grappling with family dynamics possibly influenced by those conditions.

The schools I attended did not acknowledge that a person or group of people had experienced forms of trauma that caused distress stemming from their social environments or their homes. They were not, as we now would say, trauma informed.[17] A trauma-informed setting raises awareness among educators or those working with students who might need a deeper level of care and concern regarding behavior or trauma responses.[18]

When educators are trauma informed, they are equipped to implement trauma-informed pedagogy that helps the educator to be aware of how their teaching practices impact students in real time. This awareness enables educators to create safe, supportive, responsive, and inclusive learning spaces and environments that address students' needs while encouraging growth. It requires a careful balance between cultivating awareness of students' experiences while maintaining academic rigor.

Additionally, it is important to distinguish between trauma-informed care and trauma-informed pedagogy, as they are related but distinctly different approaches:

- ***Trauma-informed care*** originated in clinical fields to meet the needs of trauma survivors, centering on principles such as safety, trust, collaboration, empowerment, and cultural responsiveness.[19]

- ***Trauma-informed pedagogy*** builds on these principles by adapting them to educational settings. It focuses on teaching practices, curriculum design, and policies that support student learning while actively working to minimize retraumatization within the classroom.[20]

By integrating these approaches, educators can create an environment where all students can thrive academically while feeling understood and supported.

When I was reading and researching, I came across the information in the table Four *R*s of Trauma-Informed Care.

However, to build on this foundational framework, I propose that four additional steps be included to expand an educator's,

FOUR *R*s OF TRAUMA-INFORMED CARE[1]

Realize—Understanding the widespread impact of trauma and recognizing potential paths to recovery.

Recognize—Identifying the signs and symptoms of trauma in clients, families, staff, and others involved with the system.

Respond—Fully integrating trauma knowledge into policies, procedures, and practices.

Resist Retraumatization—Actively working to prevent retraumatization of both children and the adults who support them.

---

[1] Jessica D. Bartlett and Kate Steber, "How to Implement Trauma-Informed Care to Build Resilience to Childhood Trauma," research brief, Child Trends, May 9, 2019, www.childtrends.org/publications/how-to-implement-trauma-informed -care-to-build-resilience-to-childhood-trauma.

FOUR ADDITIONAL Rs OF TRAUMA-INFORMED CARE

Reflect—It starts with reflection, taking a moment to look inward, to examine our own attitudes, actions, and biases that might affect those who've experienced trauma. Reflecting on ourselves lays the groundwork for the *Realize* step of trauma-informed care, helping us understand the broader impact of trauma by first understanding our role within it.

Respect—Then comes respect. Acknowledging the individuality of each person's experiences and boundaries is essential. Respect builds on the *Recognize* step, as it requires us to go beyond simply noticing signs of trauma to truly honoring the humanity of each person. This respect creates a safe, supportive community where people feel seen and valued, a critical part of any trauma-informed approach.

Restore—After respect, there's a need to restore. This is about actively creating healing environments that encourage resilience, contributing to the *Respond* step. Just as responding means integrating trauma-informed practices, restoring focuses on building spaces that encourage recovery and peace, helping students move forward in a supportive, community-centered, nurturing environment.

Reconnect—Finally, reconnect. Trauma often isolates people and students, disrupting relationships and community ties. The *Resist Re-traumatization* step involves avoiding harm, but reconnecting goes one step further, building relationships that empower and uplift a person or student who may have journeyed through trauma. Reconnection means helping people rebuild trust and a sense of belonging, creating a community of support that carries them toward healing and strength.

school's, and community's awareness and response. These are outlined in the table Four Additional Rs of Trauma-informed Care.

The turmoil of my childhood and the context in which I was raised fit into a larger societal framework. The challenges I faced were not isolated incidents but part of a broader pattern shaped by systemic factors and personal trauma intertwined. These factors can influence the life paths of many people who emerged from the same types of environments as I did. For countless Black and Brown students growing up in similar conditions across the country, the narrative is all too familiar. However, we must continue to seek to understand all the complexities of those trying to find social, emotional, and educational health. In neighborhoods where the stains of hardship reverberate through the streets, many carry the invisible burden of adverse childhood experiences, just as I did. These young souls face the same internal, social, and relentless battles against the tides of systemic injustices and family turmoil. Their stories woven into the fabric of historical injustice and oppressed communities nationwide speak to a shared struggle and attest to the resilience required to navigate a world that seems predisposed to their experiencing injustice and disenfranchisement long before they have a chance to reach higher education.

A MOMENT OF REFLECTION

The African symbol of the sankofa is a bird with its head turned backward and its body facing forward. The word *sankofa* breaks down into three words: *san* means "return," *ko* means "go," and *fa* means "to look, seek, and take." The word suggests that we must never forget where we came from—or what has shaped us.

Reflecting on and reclaiming the lessons from our past as a society and using this process to understand my own growth required significant inner work. This effort empowers us collectively to recognize the type of work needed to ensure that children, youth, young adults, and adults who have been harmed and traumatized by their social conditions receive the support they need. This support is crucial for them to navigate their challenges in a healthy way, ensuring that their educational or goal journeys are not adversely affected in the future.

Pause for a moment and put yourself in the shoes of someone born into an environment riddled with violence or material and social poverty. Imagine constant transition, moving from place to place with fear of more violence following you. Consider the weight, the emotional heaviness, the challenge of processing complex feelings without guidance, and the impact this might have on your ability to focus on a classroom. Could you have survived school? Would you have been able to engage with your studies, make friends, or even envision a future for yourself? Did you experience this yourself?

Now, think about the millions who face these types of barriers and injustices daily, much like the people Howard Thurman describes in his prophetic book *Jesus and the Disinherited*. These are people like me, like my mother and some of my family and people in my community—people with their backs against the wall, navigating social conditions and personal challenges shaped by systemic oppression in a world that often seems indifferent to their struggles, while also being hostile toward those whose skin has been kissed by nature's sun. When you process this, ask yourself: Is this also my story? What did I need? What is needed to ensure that people who grow up in environments with their backs against the wall are able to grow and not wither? However, there are ways in which to flourish and break through the concrete, and we will see what it takes.

THREE

AIN'T GOT NO PENCIL

After my ninth birthday and with my mother's permission, my dad began to be present more consistently in my life again. A sports enthusiast, my dad saw it as his responsibility to introduce me to football. Those are still some of my best memories with my dad because I believe that is where I learned a lot of leadership skills that I display in my life's work today. I remember my first induction into the game of football. One afternoon, my dad picked me up to go to a sports store, where I tried on football equipment. As a novice with no knowledge of the sport, I felt a mixture of excitement and nervousness. However, my desire to be close to my dad overcame any apprehensions. The store clerk helped me try on shoulder pads, pants, knee pads, and the rest of the necessary gear. Unaware that different positions require different helmets, I selected a bulky and very unsuitable defensive lineman helmet—after all I didn't even know what position I would play, or if I would be any good at all.

At the time, Ben Hill Recreation Center had organized a summer football camp and practice, drawing in hundreds of students and youth from the community.[1] Sometimes, when I pass by groups of elementary, middle, or high school students practicing on the fields near my home, I can't help but reminisce about my first day at camp. Despite my lack of experience, one of the recreational coaches, whom we called Coach Kool-Aid, noticed my potential and made me a defensive end due to my solid footwork, eventually moving me to a cornerback position. My role, however, quickly expanded. The following summer, I spent more time with Coach Kool-Aid and Coach Cowan, who recognized my strong throwing arm. By the start of the season, I was the quarterback for our recreational team and even led us to the championship. We didn't win, but I was a leader. For the next three years, I dedicated myself to this position, learning invaluable leadership lessons that I still apply today—lessons like gathering people, speaking up, leading through loss, and one of the greatest lessons, using my voice.

I discovered the significance of hard work and persistence. Whatever the challenges, I learned to keep pushing forward. When faced with setbacks, I found the strength to get back up. And when someone criticized me or yelled at me, I saw it as an opportunity to become better. In addition to the skills and lessons I learned from football, the sport also helped me understand the power of community. I still miss those end-of-season banquets where team members gathered to celebrate our accomplishments—we all received trophies. The trophies were plastic, but they reminded us that we were all worth the time and effort our coaches and community poured into us. The camaraderie and the sense of being a part of something greater than myself were truly special. That was the beauty of the Campbellton Road community; it provided support, a sense of togetherness, family, and guidance—even when there were community problems and times got tough for families.

Yet the harsher sides of our reality were never far away. During Little League football and baseball practices, Coach Kool-Aid (who played football for Grambling State University, a historically Black college and university—HBCU) used to say, "Not everyone is lucky enough to make it out." What he meant was that not everyone escapes the neighborhood with a solid education, a successful career, or the kind of personal growth and confidence that would enable them to transcend an environment riddled with poverty. In fact, he once told a few players from the team, "The reality is that some of you might not finish school or have the best path out of the hood. That will depend on how you take what we are teaching you and use it to overcome." He understood trauma awareness long before any of us had sophisticated language to identify it, recognizing the deep emotional impacts of living in poverty and how it shapes one's mental and emotional well-being. But I understood exactly what he was talking about.

My coach shared these words in the early 1990s, around the time of the Rodney King beating, and talked to us about the obvious poverty and urban blight in Black neighborhoods. And the reality is that much of what I experienced when I was growing up remains true for many today. Coach dedicated himself to serving the youth after he overcame the odds and attended college.

THE TRAUMA OF POVERTY

Children navigating the dual realities of being both students and impoverished community members often carry burdens that extend far beyond the visible deprivations of their living conditions. Poverty is a multifaceted and intersectional force, violently impacting not only the financial stability of families with children who are students living in these poor communities but also the child's soul and psyche. Growing up in environments overwhelmed with scarcity, injustice, family disruptions, and trauma exposes a form of poverty that transcends economic deficiency.

Rev. William J. Barber II, leader of the Poor People's Campaign, has publicly spoken about the violence of poverty when he said that it is a death sentence for anyone who lives in it without being able to escape its clutches. He says that poverty claims "the lives of 800 people a day."[2] Pause for a moment and take in what you just read while also considering the impact of poverty not solely on adults but on young students who will wrestle with poverty generationally when they are adults. Some people will literally have their lives and academic and living potential cut off not because they lack the potential but because poverty is so violent that the lack of proper resources can cause both a metaphorical and literal death. Rev. Barber has often stated in his lectures that he believed that some people do not die prematurely because God has called them home; some people die prematurely because they are poor and do not have what they need to survive or are low wealth.[3]

When I hear these words, I am reminded of my own journey—as a young boy, as a teenager, and as a young adult—trying to become a Black man. I reflect on navigating a brief period of being unhoused and living on the streets due to the social and familial poverty we experienced. It was a challenging time in my life, as I worked to find both myself and a positive path forward. I also hear what is not being spoken—the trauma of waking up and not knowing where your food is coming from, trying to find shelter, affording a place to stay on minimum wages, wondering how you will wash your child's socks. What Rev. Barber is saying is that without proper access, it is hard to live a full life.

Barber's outcry is warranted, especially after the research that the Institute for Policy Studies, in partnership with the Poor People's Campaign, Kairos, and Repairers of the Breach, revealed in their report *The Souls of Poor Folk*: 140 million people in the United States are considered poor, with a disproportionate number being Black and Brown, while significant research backs up this data and states that poverty itself is the fourth leading cause of death in the United States.[4] The report details how persistent poverty, systemic racism, the war economy, and ecological devastation, when they intersect, can exacerbate the struggles faced by the poor, stripping those born into such conditions of basic necessities required for survival. For instance, the war economy refers to a system where excessive military spending and priorities drain resources from essential social programs, exacerbating poverty and inequality.[5] Additionally, on an educational level, these factors impact the daily lives of students who come from deeply deprived environments. Poverty becomes a form of violence that strips away everything necessary to ensure a person's well-being. Therefore, poverty is inherently traumatic.

While poverty and trauma are two distinct things, substantial research and evidence show that when social conditions are poor, it can hinder growth and development, impact long-term health outcomes, increase stress, and has been known to cause PTSD. Therefore, it is reasonable to conclude that the environment itself can be considered traumatic for anyone living in those conditions. Coreen Knowles, however, makes an interesting point that poverty in many ways is not seen as a type of trauma. She suggests:

> Without seeing poverty as a type of trauma well-meaning helpers may very well be missing crucial aspects of what a person actually needs, both in terms of concrete resources and for healing. If we could broaden our focus regarding trauma and include living in poverty as a potentially traumatic event, we could both better serve people living in poverty and likely be more effective in advocating for prevention and systematic change.[6]

Her scholarship helps us understand the link between poverty and trauma, and I would add that there is also a broader connection that includes systemic injustices that target communities of color and concentrated poverty in communities where trauma itself becomes the shared experience, making the duo of poverty and trauma particularly destructive. Other research has explored the clear links between structural racism—encompassing poverty, income inequality, and disempowering and discriminatory economic structures—and wellness and health outcomes, including the effects of trauma.[7] So instead of seeing poverty and trauma as separate as in the following diagram, it is intertwined as in the diagram underneath it.

Understanding this link also helps us recognize the social conditions that impact educational outcomes and challenges. In the Generational Trauma and Educational Inequity Framework (see the introduction), I illustrate the linear connection that becomes a cycle. I do this to reveal the interconnection of multiple factors, while also highlighting how these issues are layered and compounding. As a scholar, I suggest we ask, Why is this important to know? Because poverty and trauma do more than affect life circumstances: they can alter how a person thinks, makes decisions, perceives the world, and understands their place in it. This is especially true when these two are linked to systemic injustice or educational injustice. This is also true when applied to students who experience both challenges and are expected to succeed in educational environments while simultaneously navigating these complex life issues.

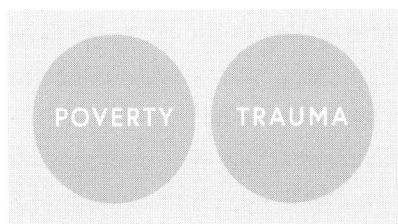

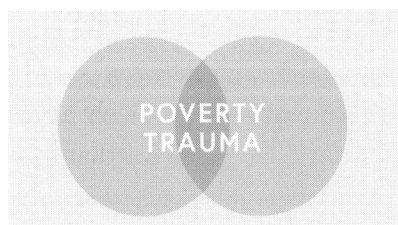

Poverty is a thief that steals potential and inflicts suffering on its victims. It leads to the decay of structures and the withering of life that leaves behind a wilderness of dryness and despair. When we recognize poverty as a form of trauma, we can begin to understand its severe impact on the well-being of students, just as I experienced. As I wrote in *I See You*, "Poverty is a lack of access."[8] Ignoring the complex and intersecting forms of violence that poverty inflicts is a disservice to those living in these conditions—a reality I am intimately familiar with—and also overlooks the significant burden poverty places on the student aspiring to excel academically.

POVERTY AFFECTS EVERYTHING

From an early age, the harsh realities of poverty impacted my understanding of the world and the community I grew up in. I believe it was partly because poverty produces such heavy trauma that studies have shown it can impact the brain itself. A study at Washington University School of Medicine examined the impact of poverty and trauma on brain development in children. It was discovered that poverty not only affects a child's behavior but also can fundamentally alter brain health and function. This is especially true when poverty is seen as a form of trauma. This team of scholars writes:

> Numerous studies of children in the US across decades have shown striking correlations between poverty and less-than-optimal physical and mental health and developmental outcomes. Trauma, poor health care, inadequate nutrition, and increased exposures to psychosocial stress and environmental toxins—all of which have significant negative developmental impacts—are likely to be involved.[9]

Dr. Kevin Johnson, who has also written extensively about the relationship between poverty and trauma, reports that such conditions can deeply impact self-esteem, educational success, and mental health and also lead to a life filled with injustice, discrimination, prejudice, and unequal opportunities. Johnson further explains how poverty can cause persistent trauma and, without adequate support, can make it difficult to navigate and recover emotionally. He also notes that poverty leads to chronic stress, which negatively affects every aspect of human functioning, particularly memory, brain development, and emotional regulation.[10] These conclusions show how poverty can be a multilayered experience.

This multilayered nature of poverty moved Coretta Scott King, wife of Dr. Martin Luther King Jr., to thoughtfully consider its real-time effects on people and communities. She emphasized the numerous ways that poverty manifests itself as violence in society by saying so famously, "I must remind you that starving a child is violence. Neglecting school children is violence. Punishing a mother and her family is violence. Discrimination against a working man is violence. Ghetto housing is violence. Ignoring medical needs is violence. Contempt for poverty is violence."[11]

King's words remind us that poverty isn't just a singular experience; it affects people emotionally, socially, environmentally, educationally, occupationally, relationally, intellectually, and in terms of their mental health. As Knowles argues, poverty is trauma itself.[12]

MY PERFECT SCORE

My first encounter with the term *adverse childhood experiences* (ACEs) occurred when I was in my midtwenties during my second year in a graduate school counseling program. At the time, I was working with at-risk middle schoolers coming out of poverty. My introduction to the ACEs Quiz, a critical test that measures emotional abuse, neglect, and other difficult childhood indicators, offered me a framework to understand and quantify the deep-seated effects of poverty and trauma that I and these students had experienced.

My professor, who was teaching a course on group therapy/counseling focused on group dynamics, introduced us to an intensive method of learning. This required not only engaging with the coursework but also participating in a group designed to cultivate a healthy dynamic among these future clinical and school counselors through dyads, triads, and whole-group interactions. I was paired with people from across the country, a few of whom I remain close to today. Our task was to become vulnerable and create a safe space to explore past traumas while taking turns facilitating the group. Before we began, our professor addressed the class, stating, "Many of you have had a number of adverse childhood experiences, and confronting these experiences may help you decide if counseling is the right path for you." His words made me reflect on my own challenging upbringing. I felt a mix of fear and curiosity about what these adverse childhood experiences would reveal.

As we got deeper into our group work, which included spending extensive hours each day exploring our pasts, many of us encountered memories that allowed us to process deeply. This was the moment I recognized how navigating poverty, trauma, and challenging social conditions had nearly prevented me from finishing high school, pursuing graduate studies, or even acquiring essential counseling skills to serve those who, like me, were enduring similar paths. The ACEs test opened my eyes to the extent of what I had overcome, informing me that poverty encompasses more than just economic struggles: it is littered with both systemic and personal trauma. When I took the ACEs Quiz, each of the ten questions brought back vivid memories of verbal abuse, physical violence, neglect, exposure to substance abuse, and mental health challenges. It revealed a picture of my formative years and the toll systematic and personal trauma, as a result of poverty, had had on me. During my childhood and all through school, I had carried fear, anger, and resentment deep within me, and I couldn't even articulate why. This realization was eye-opening for me.

ACES QUIZ

The ACEs quiz is more than just a set of questions—it's a window into the deep and often hidden impacts from a person's early life, especially a life marked by trauma, poverty, violence, and systemic injustice. Many clinicians view this as a tool to uncover the types of difficult or traumatic experiences that a child may have endured in these environments, as these experiences not only affect early life but also have the power to shape the landscape of a person's mental health, emotional well-being, and overall wellness that can follow them into adulthood. Even though there are only ten questions in that test, they rocked me and are very direct. They ask things like, Did you face emotional or physical abuse, such as being yelled at or hurt by an adult in your household? Were there moments of sexual abuse involving an older person or instances of sexual assault by someone outside your family? Did you feel neglected, lacking essentials like food, clothing, or access to medical care and help when you needed it most?[13]

But the ACEs Quiz doesn't stop at personal experiences; it also probes the environment itself and examines those who shared it with you—particularly household dynamics. It asks about the mental health of those living with you, substance abuse, witnessing domestic violence, or experiencing a family member being imprisoned. It unpacks relationship dynamics and addresses the pain of parental separation or loss, whether through divorce, death, abandonment, or other reasons.[14]

When you score high on the ACEs test, it indicates significant exposure to multiple layers of adversity that can shape a person's life and follow them throughout their developmental years. Research has shown that these scores are associated with heightened health risks in adulthood, pose challenges for social well-being and educational achievement, and underscore that the impacts of childhood adversity are profound and enduring. These effects reach beyond mere memories, influencing physical and mental health, resilience, and the overall trajectory of one's life.[15]

10 OUT OF 10

Scoring 10 out of 10 on the ACEs Quiz was a sobering moment for me. It wasn't just a number; it was a reflection of the tumultuous journey I had been on since childhood. As my friend Dr. Jerome Lubbe, DC, DACNB, a functional neurologist, explained to me:

> Each yes you answer on this test can be seen as a negative number (encounter), effectively lowering you into a pit created by damaging and/or life-threatening experiences. You must then work to climb out of this pit just to reach emotionally stable ground. In reality, the higher your ACE score, the more your body has to overcome. You don't get to be fragile or fatigue easily. Every yes on your ACE test will cultivate a stronger relationship with pain than your counterparts with lower scores. Ultimately, the individual with a higher ACE score will develop the muscles of resilience in a way that only survival strategies could create.[16]

The adverse experiences that Dr. Lubbe talks about explain why I say that each yes I answered brought back the moments when I felt a sense of invisibility within my own family, the fear I experienced from witnessing physical violence, and all the days I watched my mom fight to ensure that my sister and I had our basic needs met. This is the trauma from poverty I experienced. For me, it explained the anger and fear that became my constant companions and revealed the emotions that I thought were just part of who I was. Acknowledging that score made me see that my struggles in school, my difficulty in forming healthy relationships, and my internal battles weren't failings on my part but scars from wounds inflicted very early in my life. And they weren't just external wounds but internal ones as well. That perfect score of mine was a painful affirmation of my past trauma, but it also became the first step in understanding the depth of my resilience and the beginning of my journey toward healing, as I overcame many barriers to reach the educational progress I attained when, statistically, I was destined to fail.

Looking deeper into my perfect ACE score, I found that some researchers have argued for expanding the ACEs framework to better capture the experiences of people of color, underscoring how structural racism amplifies personal trauma. This research uncovered a critical gap in early ACEs research and its failure to fully account for the experiences of people of color, particularly in how structural racism exacerbates trauma.[17] Their insights resonated deeply with me, offering a broader lens through which to view my perfect ACE score from the social location I emerged from in the 1980s and 1990s. It was no longer just a measure of personal adversity but also a reflection of a broader, systemic issue that disproportionately affects Black and Brown people and communities.

The history of ACEs traces its origins to a quiet street in San Diego at an obesity clinic operated by Kaiser Permanente's Department of Preventive Medicine. In 1985, Department Chief Dr. Vincent Felitti faced a perplexing issue. Over half of the participants in his obesity clinic were dropping out annually, despite successfully losing weight. This mystery launched Felitti on a twenty-five-year quest in collaboration with researchers from the Centers for Disease Control and involved more than seventeen thousand members of Kaiser Permanente's San Diego care program. The study unearthed that adverse childhood experiences were alarmingly common, even among the clinic's predominantly White, middle-class demographic, and that these experiences were linked to major chronic illnesses and social problems plaguing the United States, with significant economic costs.[18]

The original study's focus and demographic did not specifically consider the experiences of Black people or other marginalized groups. This lack of consideration revealed a significant gap in early ACEs research, as it may not have fully represented the complexities and additional adversities faced by these communities, including systemic racism, discrimination, and economic gaps.[19]

Understanding the history of ACEs and its initial limitations helped me to see not only the complexities of poverty and its relationship to trauma but also the extra layers of weight added to understanding my Blackness and the societal backdrop that included unique, compounded pressure.

CAUSE I AIN'T GOT A PENCIL

In April 2014, educator Joshua T. Dickerson was inspired to write a poem titled "Cause I Ain't Got a Pencil" after witnessing an incident involving a student who asked his teacher for a pencil in an Atlanta school, realizing he did not have one. Instead of being socially aware and trauma informed, the teacher proceeded to ask the student to exchange one of his shoes for a pencil. Dickerson described what happened next as "heartbreaking" and said it became the inspiration for the now-viral poem. In an interview, Dickerson shared that, "The child took off the shoe and he had a dirty sock on, and it caused the other students in the class to laugh at him . . . I wrote a story about what I imagined happened prior to that moment."[20]

Dickerson went on to explain that students navigating a community with concentrated poverty and underresourced schools could find themselves wrestling not only with their living conditions outside school but also with those challenges following them while trying to excel academically. The poem itself explores the depths of what any student in such circumstances would have to endure while revealing the story behind the student's simple request for a pencil from a teacher.

I woke myself up
Because we ain't got an alarm clock

Dug in the dirty clothes basket,
Cause ain't nobody washed my uniform
Brushed my hair and teeth in the dark,
Cause the lights ain't on
Even got my baby sister ready,
Cause my mama wasn't home.
Got us both to school on time,
To eat us a good breakfast.
Then when I got to class the teacher fussed
Cause I ain't got no pencil.[21]

My first time reading both the story and the poem resulted in a flood of tears. It just reminded me so much of my own childhood. I too remember the laughter of my peers when I attended classes wearing older shoes, hand-me-down clothes, and knock-off brands from the flea market, items my mother and sometimes my father bought because we couldn't afford anything else. I also remember the social climate we lived in and how poverty was a constant burden on my mother. I know that the weight of those experiences shaped me as a student.

Dickerson's poem brilliantly and painfully captures the depths of poverty in a way that helps people understand that poverty isn't just a surface-level experience or just about the lack of a pencil. It communicates that poverty's reach extends beyond the lack of material goods in front of you and can create educational barriers. The child's dirty sock is evidence of the lack of a washing machine and the struggle of the child's family, which results in a lack of support from peers in the classroom and the teacher's failure to understand the real reasons the student came unprepared. Poverty, which can also be social in nature, shows up in this poem through the lack of empathy in the laughter of the other students. All this likely added to the emotional pain this student must have felt, through no fault of their own. One can clearly see that poverty carries with it the weight of numerous burdens that make schooling challenging for students navigating these realities when they converge simultaneously.

My heart went out to this student and to the countless other children who enter schools where educators are unaware of all that was being carried by the children and how their living conditions affect their performance. When an educator is not aware or trauma informed, they can only see the surface of students without recognizing the myriad obstacles they have overcome just to appear in a classroom. Their lack of awareness can cause missed opportunities for the educator to care in ways that are more supportive of their students—even if it is providing connection to resources.

THE STORY BEHIND THE STUDENT

Student's classroom presence—When a student walks into a class, their presence alone does not provide educators with the depth of understanding needed to comprehend the stories the student might be carrying internally or from their social location. When a teacher or educator solely relies on presence, a lot can be overlooked in a student's holistic circumstances.

Student's home life—A student's presence in class doesn't fully reveal the challenges this student faces at home. When a teacher or educator is unaware or ignores these signs, it causes them to respond with a "What's wrong with you?" instead of with a "What's happened or happening to you?" approach, which could impact the student and the ways that educator could aid the student.

Student's social environment or social stigmas—A student's social environment might also contribute to the stories they carry with them into the school setting. They could emerge from an environment of battling stigma, facing urban hassles, dealing with problems at home, or navigating situations that exacerbate their

experiences with poverty and trauma. When an educator overlooks this, they miss an opportunity to build a bridge and relational depth with the student to make the student feel safe.

Student's lived experiences—Each student could be bringing experiences from their home and social context into the classroom that
have caused trauma and impacted their ability to focus. Understanding this could help the educator or teacher mobilize the
proper support to aid the student where the student is cared for
with a holistic approach.

Student's emotional impact from lived experiences—Both social and
emotional impacts could create barriers for the student, affecting
how they connect with education and feel safe in their learning
environment. Understanding this is crucial in that schools that
have a high concentration of poverty should advocate for more
support and accommodations for students who have these types
of challenges.

A deeper look: Layers of experience and impact

It's important to recognize the various layers of impact here. A student's
presence in the classroom is just one aspect of their educational experience.
This presence is distinct from their home life, social environment, and
lived experiences. These factors, while unique to each student, intersect
and contribute to the emotional impact that a student incurs as a result of
these cumulative experiences. Together, they compose the complex reality
of the whole student—each layer influencing how the student engages
with their education and peers. This nuanced understanding is crucial for
educators and support systems aiming to address the full spectrum of
challenges that students may face.

ADVOCATING FOR STUDENTS FROM SYSTEMICALLY
DISADVANTAGED BACKGROUNDS

I fear that we have forgotten the heaviness and trauma that ac-
companies poverty when it comes to understanding the educational challenges of students who may still find themselves wrestling with poverty around the country and even the world. I fear

we have not given our all as a society to ensure that students who are journeying through this reality feel safe enough to show up to learn, regardless of the stories they bring from their living conditions. We must remember that poverty is violent, and it is my belief that *we need not only more trauma-informed schools and informed educators and pedagogy but also the freedom to create more safe spaces and support for students.* This support could consist of students not being in fear of punishment or embarrassment if they don't have a pencil or show up in dirty socks, but *it could also take the form of more concern being shown for the student's stories beyond the classroom.* It is my belief that understanding poverty as a form of trauma is crucial in creating the support and resources needed to change the trajectories of those who face built-in barriers due to their social environments and the lack of access to essential support and sustainable opportunities. We must have the poverty conversation when it comes to education because poverty itself is a large reason why many people are fighting on a path that is already designed for their academic failure.

And because I have a faith tradition that I claim, it is also my ethical responsibility to challenge those who identify as Christian, or as following any faith tradition, to wrestle with the concepts of being trauma informed. We must not ignore the ways in which poverty, historical trauma, and social living conditions can impact people and their educational trajectories. Christians in particular are often not trauma informed and tend to use faith language to rush people past their experiences with trauma, which can lead to religious trauma. Instead, Christians must learn how to create stable environments that provide spaces for people to heal and flourish.

Yet, when we look at the life and ministry of Jesus, we see a model of what it means to be deeply attuned to the pain and experiences of others—we see a clear model of this practice, even in the midst of his own experiences with trauma. For example, Jesus experienced displacement, a form of trauma, when King Herod issued a decree to eliminate male children under age two, forcing his family to flee to Egypt for safety (Matthew 2:13-15). He faced labeling, another form of trauma, as he was dismissed as merely the carpenter's son (Matthew 13:55) and questioned—"Can anything good come from Nazareth?" (John 1:46). He was even called unwell and accused of being "out of his mind" (Mark 3:21). When he returned to Nazareth, he faced rejection and disbelief from those who had known him since childhood (Luke 4:16-30). Despite this personal rejection, he continued to preach the good news, embodying resilience and compassion.

From his compassionate engagement with the woman at the well to his gentle care for the man suffering from being possessed, Jesus consistently recognized the humanity of those who were hurting and responded with love, dignity, and healing. The Gospels are filled with moments when Jesus meets people in their trauma, creating spaces of safety and solidarity. His approach was one of deep awareness, showing us that being trauma informed is not only practical but profoundly like the historical Jesus of Nazareth.

Poverty transcends mere financial deprivation but is connected directly to social, environmental, and generational trauma. Social trauma exists and it can hinder those who find themselves trapped in environments that were seemingly designed for them to fail. This itself creates educational barriers and challenges for many students. It is my hope that we get to a place where we start to see poverty as an evil force that claims lives and hinders brilliant minds from reaching the heights of higher education—and may we be moved to do something about it long before students say, "cause I ain't got no pencil."

A MOMENT OF REFLECTION

When I finally realized how trauma and poverty in my own life were so indelibly linked, I broke down in tears, but it also became the step toward healing that I needed. What if we created a world where more people could heal without shame? This understanding of the emotional journey that I had endured to feel safe, to believe in myself, and to pursue higher education despite poverty making me feel inadequate, was a long and hard-fought journey. Can you recall your own journey if you've experienced this? The depth, the resilience, and the barriers that still exist?

We need to pause and reflect on poverty as violence and challenge ourselves on how we can view poverty not only with more compassion but also as a multilayered stack of barriers that are difficult, but not impossible, to overcome. Only by recognizing these complexities can we begin to dismantle the structures and systems that perpetuate poverty and support those striving to break free from its grasp and from educational injustice.

Consider how many challenges a person must navigate in their environment to achieve emotional stability. Think about the barriers some face in the community before even leaving home. How do these experiences shape a person's outlook on life, aspirations, and resilience in the face of adversity? Were these systemic barriers intentionally designed to hold people back from achieving all they could become?

But more importantly, what role could you play in responding to these inequities and altering these sad trajectories? What might you, your institution, or your community do to help address these conditions?

FOUR

DROPOUT BY DESIGN?

I recently had a conversation with my older sister Dr. Monica Lester, a clinical social worker in the DC area. She helped me reflect on my childhood and upbringing. "Do you have any good childhood memories?" she asked.

I still feel the chills and the surge of emotions from that question. "Only a couple," I responded. When my parents were together, my dad would walk me to the end of the street to play video games at a nearby convenience store and allow me to get some candy. I can still remember walking into that store with him when I was four years old, the smell of the freshly mopped floor, and the sound the change made as he received it from the store clerk after exchanging a dollar bill. He also coached me in sports. I can still remember those moments and, although they were brief, they felt safe and peaceful. Reflecting on the lack of good childhood memories revealed to me how much I was depleted and starved for connection, acceptance, belonging, and care. I had longed for a sense of home in an environment historically not designed for stability.

This was surely why I chose to be literally beaten into what I perceived as a family of peers who were dealing with the same pain I was. I joined a gang, and that decision almost cost me my life.

When I was twelve, a family settled into our community off Campbellton Road, having fled the gang-afflicted streets of Los Angeles.[1] The family had two sons, Marcus and Jordan. Jordan, who was younger, began attending Ralph Bunche Middle School with me. I befriended him, and we seemed to bond over our mutual pain, how our fathers were not at home, and our neighborhood's poverty.

I'm assuming the parents thought that a move would change their sons. But because they had been exposed to gang culture in LA, that experience never left them, making it difficult to change. They introduced gang culture to our middle school community while other gangs were beginning to take over the neighborhood. As the influence of gang culture grew in our community and school, gang initiations became more prevalent across the city.[2] Soon, I joined the gang they had been part of in LA.

My initiation was brutal. I was beaten severely in a restroom with the lights off by fifteen of my peers, an experience that oddly mirrored the violence I had witnessed at home. This type of trauma, coupled with the poverty I endured, led me to form what can only be described as a trauma bond with the gang culture, a bond that many researchers link to the economic and social pressures that drive youth toward gang membership.[3] It seemed that I was seeking some type of connection through shared hardship and a misguided attempt to belong. Soon I felt I was beginning to finally have a sense of family and solidarity with people who made gang life seem like an answer to the disruption of home and scarcity.

After I joined the gang, my life began to head down the inevitable path to destruction. My academic performance plummeted as I struggled to navigate the complex emotions and social challenges I faced as a part of a gang. As I grew older, the disconnect between my home life and school experience worsened. My engagement with the emerging hip-hop culture of the nineties resonated with the emotional pain I was feeling, and by the end of tenth grade, my struggles had culminated in an arrest where I was facing two felony charges. Although these were eventually dropped, I continued to descend down a dangerous path. As eleventh grade approached, I had fallen so far behind because I was dealing with PTSD from my childhood, lost interest in school, and started being influenced by the social context that was systematically created for my material and inner poverty.

I lost any desire to continue my education. When you carry a lot of heaviness inside and battle external and systemic issues, sometimes it is hard to connect with the world around you without feeling empty, especially in school. The more I was unable to connect with the school setting, the more I failed classes, and I fell further and further behind.

The new pressures of the wrong associations, created and exacerbated by the unstable, impoverished environment, conspired to drain my attention away from school. My experience, however, also reflects Jawanza Kunjufu's discourse on the systemic biases against Black boys. Kunjufu's *Countering the Conspiracy to Destroy Black Boys*, written in 1985, reveals a disturbing trend that was happening when I was growing up.[4] He wrote in a time period when society was predicting the building of prisons that would be populated with Black men based on the test scores of Black boys as early as third grade, a narrative further validated in *The New Jim Crow*.[5]

In a public lecture on countering the conspiracy, Kunjufu explained the harsh reality of what causes a Black male student to go from being deeply engaged to not being engaged at all because of the shift in the interest of education of young Black boys as they move through elementary school. Part of that disinterest is grounded in the way Black boys are not engaged in their imaginations as children, and it starts to fade away when it is not nurtured and influenced by cultural trends and systemic issues. The disengagement could be triggered by multiple environmental hardships and trying to cope with lack, social pressures, being labeled and stereotyped, lack of representation in the curriculum or at home, as well as an inability to see beyond their immediate environment. He also told an audience in 1987 that we must consider, "When did the conspiracy start? Who is against Black boys? Why is there a conspiracy against them? What exactly is the conspiracy?" He made the powerful statement that "if you can destroy Black boys, they will never become Black men."[6] And while Kunjufu was a scholar talking about these things in the 1980s, his conclusions came through the unique lens of a sociologist, a scholar, and a father who helped raise Black children himself and witnessed the targeting of Black communities and Black men through public policy.

While Kunjufu's work primarily focused on Black males, it also critically examined three pivotal areas relevant to the Black experience of the eighties and what I faced as a child dealing with these intersectional experiences.[7] Reflecting on his work—particularly his research on the targeting of young Black males during this time period—I recognize that, as a young Black man myself, I was the very subject of his studies. I find it difficult to process the complex dynamics that made it challenging for me and others to navigate these same roads, especially considering the decades leading up to the twenty-first century. As an adult, it is heavy seeing how generational trauma, systemic barriers, and the misuse of power all worked together to hinder my potential and that of others just like me in the form of educational injustice. Knowing the immense barriers they are up against, how can children be expected to focus on schoolwork when their home life or living environment has a traumatic weight that disconnects them from their own life?

TOO FAR BEHIND

One day, my mother and I were asked to have a serious conversation at the high school about the trouble I had gotten into and to talk about the slim chance I had of any academic success. This meeting was with the assistant principal Mr. Hughes, who was responsible for monitoring the progress of the class I was supposed to graduate with. I walked into that office, bracing myself to hear the worst about myself and my grim future.

Sitting across from Mr. Hughes, I will never forget the first words that came out of his mouth to my mother: "I don't have such good news about your son. We have to have an honest conversation about Terence's ability to excel." And then the next few words felt like all the years of the systemic failure and poverty I was a part of collided and came down on me all at once.

"I don't think you will be able to finish school here, Terence. You have fallen too far behind."

Hearing those words that I would not be able to finish and graduate on time added more crushing weight to what I had already carried throughout my childhood. By that time, I believed I had endured enough punishment as opposed to having teachers and educators provide me with the type of support I needed to self-regulate and understand my pain so I could flourish as a student.[8] I was now becoming a 1990s statistic. School was supposed to be a place where my psychological safety and support were top priorities, but I could not ever recall feeling that type of support as I listened to the words coming from this assistant principal. Sitting there, I had this moment where I silently wondered, *Does anyone actually care about my pain?* Up until then, it felt like I was only ever punished for my trauma and pain and never really supported through it. I can count on one hand the number of people in that school who made me feel seen.

Mr. Hughes was only partly right. By then, I had pretty much disconnected from high school. The unresolved trauma I was carrying around had created this cycle where I just couldn't find a way to tap into the potential that I knew was inside me. My mom doing her absolute best as a frustrated single parent was right there with me, her heart breaking over how things were turning out regarding my education. And Mr. Hughes? All he could really say was, "I don't know what to say, but I apologize this has happened."

It was a tough spot. Both he and I were caught up in a system that felt like it was designed to let students like me fall through the cracks. I doubt he knew he was part of a system that was all too quick to punish struggling students. Because Mr. Hughes did everything he could to give challenged students chance after chance, I truly believe his intentions were good. However, I do not think he fully understood the social locations and systemic barriers that made it significantly harder for some students to recognize and seize those chances as true opportunities. I know he didn't see the full picture of what we were going through. If he knew even half of what my life was like—the depths of what my mother carried alone and the journey we were on overcoming poverty and the effects of trauma—he just might have understood. However, I now know that my path was set long before we ever sat down in his office that day.

EDUCATIONAL REDLINING

Only when I began my graduate education did I begin to pay serious attention to a phenomenon that I term *educational redlining*. Redlining is a long-standing banking practice that blocked people of color from getting mortgages. The Student Borrower Protection Center defines it as "financial companies' use of individuals' education history to screen borrowers for loans [and] penalize borrowers of color and community college students."[9]

Researchers from the University of California, Berkeley's School of Public Health found that decades of redlining continue to perpetuate racial and socioeconomic inequality in the San Francisco Bay Area and across the country. Although illegal since 1968, redlining's harmful legacy has left Black and Brown communities struggling with air pollution, reproductive health disorders, fewer urban amenities, and significant barriers in accessing higher education.[10]

I would suggest that historical redlining within Black communities has been a major hurdle for many, including myself, because of the lasting consequences of this misuse of power and policy. And I use the term *redlining* after *educational* to help people understand the barriers in accessing higher education and the obstacles that hinder Black and Brown students from being able to afford or even qualify to enter graduate-level programs.

Educational redlining describes the systemic barriers that disproportionately limit Black and Brown communities from accessing higher education. Much like housing redlining, this practice manifests through discriminatory policies and structural inequities in loans, funding, college acceptance, GPA requirements, standardized testing, and other institutional measures that create additional hurdles for marginalized students. These barriers not only deter individuals from pursuing higher education but also reinforce long-standing educational inequities by restricting opportunities based on race, socioeconomic status, and geography.

In 2014, Ta-Nehisi Coates's article "The Case for Reparations" went viral. Published in *The Atlantic*, it detailed the egregious injustices faced by Black people, including mistreatment, land theft, and strategic exclusion from homeownership. He writes, "From the 1930s through the 1960s, black people across the country were largely cut out of the legitimate home-mortgage market." He makes the case for reparations by detailing how systemic racism has historically contributed to the exclusion of wealth for Black people. He reveals that "the income gap between black and white households is roughly the same today as it was in 1970," largely due to continuing unjust practices. To illustrate this, Coates introduces the work of Patrick Sharkey, a sociologist at New York University, who found that from 1955 to 1970, only 4 percent of White children and a staggering 62 percent of Black children in America were raised in impoverished neighborhoods. Sharkey noted, "A generation later, the same study showed, virtually nothing had changed. And whereas whites born into affluent neighborhoods tended to remain in affluent neighborhoods, blacks tended to fall out of them."[11] Coates examines redlining to illustrate how barriers to homeownership and land access have historically prevented wealth accumulation in Black communities.

Making the connection between wealth and housing also gave me an opportunity to see how the concentration of poverty could lead to affecting educational outcomes that are harsher for those who live in areas that are riddled with poverty. Coates further writes:

> Black families, regardless of income, are significantly less wealthy than white families. The Pew Research Center estimates that white households are worth roughly 20 times as much as black households, and that whereas only 15 percent of whites have zero or negative wealth, more than a third of blacks do. Effectively, the black family in America is working without a safety net. When financial calamity strikes—a medical emergency, divorce, job loss—the fall is precipitous.[12]

Dr. Richard Rothstein, in his book *The Color of Law* released three years after Ta-Nehisi Coates's article, expands on and meticulously documents the intentional and deliberate segregation of Black and White residents in the United States through public policy and de jure segregation tactics that became law so as to exclude Black people from living in certain areas.[13] The goal was to uphold segregation in housing and systematically concentrate poverty in Black communities.[14] Public housing (i.e., ghettos and projects) was initially created to provide quality housing for war veterans, which morphed into a tool for segregation solidifying both racial and economic isolation. Rothstein relates how, during World War II, Richmond, California, saw a massive influx of workers, including many Black people. Despite working side by side with White colleagues in the shipyards and factories, Black people were barred from living in White neighborhoods. The government built public housing to accommodate the surge, but it was explicitly segregated. Black people were crammed into poorly constructed temporary units near the industrial areas, while White workers got better, permanent housing farther inland. This segregation wasn't just about where people lived; it extended to social activities and community services, reinforcing racial divisions. With limited private housing options, many Black families had no choice but to move into these segregated public housing projects, which concentrated poverty and created lasting "ghettos" in the city. This same phenomenon is seen across the country.[15] Today, Black people remain in areas that lack access to good health care, housing, public services, infrastructure, job opportunities—and quality educational facilities.[16]

> Before we became ashamed to admit that the country had circumscribed African Americans in ghettos, analysts of race relations, both African American and white, consistently and accurately used ghetto to describe low-income African American neighborhoods, created by public policy, with a shortage of opportunity, and with barriers to exit.[17]

GEOGRAPHICALLY DISADVANTAGED

Understanding the impact of where we live is crucial because location, geography, and access can dramatically shape educational outcomes and opportunities, both positively and negatively. By examining the geographical makeup of communities, especially in cities like Chicago, Atlanta, and Detroit where there are significant concentrations of Black and Brown residents, we can see the direct impact of how difficult it is to afford higher education when one can barely afford to stay in a specific part of town, and why many first-generation college students come from communities that were intentionally designed to be concentrated areas of poverty. These cities often have schools funded by property taxes, which adversely affects communities that are poorer, creating a significant imbalance in school funding and a lack of exposure to levels of education for their students. NPR reported:

> The problem with a school-funding system that relies so heavily on local property taxes is straightforward: Property values vary a lot from neighborhood to neighborhood, district to district. And with them, tax revenues.
>
> To help poorer schools compensate for that local imbalance, some states have stepped in. In 2013, North Carolina provided two-thirds of its schools' funding.
>
> "If we didn't have that, we'd be in pretty dire straits right now," says Rodney Shotwell, superintendent of Rockingham County Schools, a low-income, rural district along the state's northern border with Virginia.
>
> This year, Rockingham got more than $5 million in extra state funding for its disadvantaged students. Shotwell says that money helped pay for teachers, instructional supplies, even custodians.[18]

Poverty is dehumanizing and targets bodies, intellect, brilliance, and academic potential. Cities like Atlanta are bound by the very red lines drawn on maps to divide poor neighborhoods, streets, and highways, ensuring that Black communities are separated from White communities and that poverty is concentrated in certain sections of the city. I now realize that wherever poverty is concentrated, there is greater scarcity that increases the chances of witnessing crime, higher risk for disease, targeted incarcerations, the unaffordability of college, higher risk for trauma, educational injustice, and a higher rate of survival struggles and homelessness.

The high cost of living and existing in these spaces can help us understand a recent report by *Inside Higher Ed*. The report looked at the multitude of systemic barriers that disproportionately affect Black and Brown people who aspire to achieve PhDs, particularly those emerging from environments shaped by systemic oppression and poverty. These barriers include financial, institutional, social, and underrepresentation challenges.[19] When we consider these barriers, it is easy to see how the residue of white supremacy designed into those communities made it easier for me to fail long before I had a chance to start.

The intentional design and almost surgical nature of how neighborhoods like the one I grew up in were created is overwhelming to think about in retrospect. I can now see how those barriers and the early challenges within my family, which led me to eventually drop out of high school as a young man, started decades before I found myself on Campbellton Road, being raised by a single mother.

There is a long history of trauma associated with Black educational progress that was set in motion hundreds of years ago and can be traced back to the era of enslavement, when Africans were prohibited from learning to read and harshly punished for seeking education.[20] This backdrop of systemic oppression laid the foundation for a long battle against segregated schooling epitomized by the "separate but equal" doctrine established by the *Plessy v. Ferguson* case, which was later challenged and overturned by the landmark *Brown v. Board of Education* decision on May 17, 1954.[21]

But the history reaches much farther back. During the Civil War, *Harper's Weekly* published newspaper articles about how being enslaved meant you were banned from all types of learning, unable to read, and punished for seeking education by severe beatings and even execution.[22] This continued into segregated schools with substandard educational spaces that were, in most cases, considered shacks or rundown facilities, and into watching a GI Bill get created for White war veterans to have access to education and housing, while you did not.[23]

The redlining Coates and Rothstein talk about concentrates poverty in neighborhoods, which creates both underfunded schools and a lack of Black teachers, while having the false language of an "achievement gap" that helps to create a social framing where Black students are inferior and unable to keep up. This uses language to suggest that Black students would never be as smart as their White peers.[24] The history of this is deep and carefully designed, especially when we look at how overcrowded and underfunded US classrooms were in the 1930s and 1940s, even in Atlanta. Its elementary schools for Black students had almost eighty-two students per teacher.[25] Could this be because of the strategic efforts to redline, segregate, and concentrate poverty?

THE TYRANNY OF GETTING TOUGH

Knowing this history helps us to understand the social landscape by the time we reach Black education for those of us born in the 1980s, and how this particular period experienced the long, compounded residue from white supremacy. *We entered schools that were still grappling with the aftermath of segregation and inequality.* The post–civil rights movement era was littered with structural injustices designed to limit Black success and force Black people into the lower working class in the United States. This era saw policies that disproportionately affected Black communities with unequal funding, unfair disciplinarian action, a lack of diversity in educational curricula, a gap in educational achievement, and a lack of representation for Black and Brown teachers.[26] In her book *Punished for Dreaming*, Dr. Bettina L. Love discusses how systemic injustices and educational disparities existed long before the landmark decision of *Brown v. Board of Education*, which aimed to desegregate schools in 1954. These issues escalated with the Reagan administration and the release of the 1983 document *A Nation at Risk: The Imperative for Educational Reform*.[27] She writes:

> I was born a scant four years before the release of *A Nation at Risk: The Imperative for Educational Reform*, the Reagan administration report on the state of American education. The report was crafted under the leadership of education secretary Terrel Bell, and its alarmist language about the systemic failure of American schools to provide adequate education, coupled with its emphasis on reform as a solution, cast a long and dark shadow over young Black people of my generation.
>
> ... "Getting tough" was a euphemism for "punishment," sold to the public as high-stakes testing, school choice, vouchers, charter schools, and school safety. At the same time, police officers were placed in schools along with metal detectors, police dogs, and surveillance equipment to control the students they now openly called *thugs* and *criminals*.[28]

Love argues that this report framed the perceived decline in American educational standards and became a catalyst for the reform movement in education, ushering in an era of increased accountability and standardized testing that disproportionately targeted Black students. She writes, "Eighties babies witnessed and, more important, experienced the joining of these industries— prisons and education—that expanded the prison industrial complex and created an educational system where Black children attended schools that structurally placed punishment, violence, police, standardized testing, and profits before learning."[29]

These disparities certainly helped establish the environment that made it easier for me to drop out as a teenager and have struggles dreaming of higher education as a young adult. Policies enacted under Reagan's administration led to an increase in the policing of schools in the 1980s, school closures due to funding cuts, and a loss of funding in the name of reform, which disproportionately impacted Black students by labeling them as "low performing." These widespread issues not only shaped the educational landscape on a macro level but also deeply affected the individual lives of students caught in the crossfire between "reform" and systemic neglect.

NUMBNESS AND A SEED

After the visit with the assistant principal, I looked at my high school transcripts and saw that I had failed over twenty classes. I had already attended three high schools—Cedar Grove High in Decatur, Westlake High in Atlanta, and Mays High in Atlanta—but was unable to find motivation in any of them. Clearly, there were reasons why Mr. Hughes was telling me that there was no way I would be able to catch up or even be considered "on track" to graduate with the class of 2000. It was then that Mr. Hughes spoke to my mother and me about Open Campus, which was a program of alternative schools for people who were on their last thread of rope or on the verge of dropping out of school altogether. He explained that it would be my last chance to catch up on my classes. And while he did not sound very optimistic or hopeful that I would succeed, I was able to complete a lot there. In any event, by that time in my life, it was too late—emotionally, I was too far gone.

After being asked to leave my school and told that I would not graduate on time, I was referred to this alternative school, which was called Frank McClarin High School in College Park, Georgia. Known as an open campus, it was seen as a last resort for those on the verge of dropping out or those considering the pursuit of a GED.[30] My first day enrolling there stands out in my memory. I found myself in an office with a counselor across from me who detailed how the school operated. She explained the self-paced nature of the classes and made it clear that if I didn't meet the requirements to progress, I would be asked to leave. The message was stark: either commit to what's needed or face the harsh realities of life without a high school diploma.

To be honest, I was indifferent. Every morning, as my mother dropped me off, I was overwhelmed. I now know this was from the weight of unresolved trauma, which left me feeling increasingly numb. Not even a month into attending the alternative school, I found myself ready to drop out completely.

One day, I decided that I was going to finally drop out. I was simply going to not complete the work and leave. But I was crying inside from the unresolved emotional pain I carried inside me. I saw the same pain in the eyes of the other students, who were carrying the same types of traumas. There were students who were unhoused, living from place to place; young ladies who were pregnant; and those who told me that they had experienced abuse and were still trying to heal. Many of the conversations I had only made me question why I would continue to show up at school when nothing about my education up to that point actually solved any of the problems and emotions that were swirling inside me.

One day, I pushed myself away from the desk, stood up, and walked out of the classroom, even while the teacher was sitting in front of the classroom. Three friends joined me, and we made our way to the front of the building. Overwhelmed by my emotions of sadness, realizing that I was falling behind in school, and unable to cope with the anxiety and depression, I told my friends,

"I am done." I was at a breaking point and thought the only way to deal with everything that I was carrying inside was to give up on school and myself. How could I concentrate on school while shouldering the immense stress from home?

As we distanced ourselves from the school, approximately forty yards away, a man experiencing homelessness called out to our group. I was the only one to respond. I walked away from my friends and approached him, noticing his tattered clothing and unkempt beard scattered with bits of trash. Yet I knew something was different about him because he did not ask for any money; he just smiled at me. I could feel his positive spirit, and his appearance did not bother me, nor did his housing status. I guess I just needed someone to say something to me that was uplifting.

The man stumbled toward me like he had been drinking and pointed toward the school. He asked, "Is that your school back there?"

I said, "Yes," and he held his head down. I'll never forget how his face reflected such deep shame. But in that brief moment, he said words I needed to hear: "Whatever you do, do not stop getting your education, or you will find yourself in a situation like mine. One day, you will become a leader."

This was one of the earliest times I was acknowledged as a leader—outside my father when my mother allowed him to come back into my life. He had coached me in sports for a brief time and taught me to take charge (his version of calling me a leader). However, this specific proclamation hadn't come from a teacher, the principal, or even my family; instead, it had come from a stranger who just happened to not have a home and was right in front of the school I was walking away from. That conversation impacted me deeply, and in that moment, a small hopeful thought took root—a seed that would one day blossom, suggesting that I could move beyond what I had gone through.

I had determined in my heart that education wasn't for me because I had been socially programmed to believe that my education was not worth it—because *I* was not worth it. It wasn't until that seed began to grow, sowed by that gentleman experiencing homelessness, that I was able to dream beyond my environment.

A MOMENT OF REFLECTION

Much of what I experienced, including dropping out of high school and falling behind in classes, is connected to a larger narrative of educational injustice and disenfranchisement. Why do I say this? Because external oppression often turns into internal oppression, creating personal challenges that manifest as educational disparities for those navigating systemic obstacles in our neighborhoods and oppressive social conditions. This interplay between external and internal barriers significantly impacts our educational journeys.

Take a moment to reflect on the stories and statistics of educational disparity you've encountered or may have witnessed others navigate. Have they only focused on academic metrics, or did they dive deeper into the lived experiences behind the numbers? Think about the obstacles and systemic injustices that students from historically marginalized communities navigate daily, not just in their schools but as part of a continuum that stretches back generations. How do these historical marks shape a student's view on learning, their future goals, and their resilience in the face of odds stacked against them? Consider the power of our collective recognition of this history and our concerted efforts to address their consequences with all of us moving toward a future where educational equity is a reality for all students, no matter where they come from.

FIVE

WITHOUT A ROOF

The first time that I left home and started living on the streets was right after I had decided to drop out of the alternative school. It was a tense time in the house where I lived with my mother and sister. My mother was carrying a lot, realizing that I was heading down a path she did not know how to steer me away from, all while trying her best to give my sister and me a hopeful future—often on her own. I think my personal wrong decisions regarding school, combined with my social environment, compounded trauma, and my mother's perpetual exhaustion from working hard to care for us, led to my inability to find a meaningful connection at home. Coupled with my mother's own trauma and her trying to work through it while working and taking care of my sister and me, this just seemed to all clash. I knew my mother loved me, but it came out in very tough ways, which made it difficult when I was trying to find connection.

I grew resentful and numb. There were days when my mother and I literally would not be able to talk to one another, and the anger that built up from never having any adults sit me down and help me work through my trauma caused me to implode. It got even worse when I saw my mother moving on with *her* life and begin dating again. Instead of connecting with any of the men my mother tried to get me to talk to in order to process what I was carrying internally—because she could see I was missing a male figure in my life, those potential mentors and the few counselors she could afford—I completely shut down. I didn't feel I could talk to anyone who did not recognize or show genuine concern for the pain I was carrying—or my anger wouldn't allow me to see people as caring. By this time, my mother had overcome some of her own challenges, obtained a graduate degree, and had gotten a better career. Because of these improvements in my mother's education and employment, we were also living in a better neighborhood on Cascade Road. On top of that, it felt like this new person in my mother's life was trying to replace my father, and that did not go well.

I had told my mother and grandmother that I was not going to school anymore—yes, even the recent last-chance school I had gotten into. My grandmother, Gloria York, would come to our house almost every day after I told her my decision, trying to get me to go back to school. But I refused. My mother also tried to convince me to return to school, but I just didn't have it in me. It all came to a head one night after I got home from sitting in a park gathering my thoughts. After walking into the house that night, I exchanged words with my mother.

There was absolutely no reason I should have talked to my mother disrespectfully, but I did. At the time, I just didn't have the language to articulate what I was dealing with inside. I'd never developed that skill. During this incident, the person my mother was dating was present and he decided to interfere. We got into a fight right there in the hallway close to my room. We tussled, and I kept yelling out, "You all just do not understand the pain I feel! You are not my father!" It was intense, and the fight escalated. My mother was distraught and he threatened to call the police. I was distraught, too, because I did not understand what was happening emotionally inside me.

The next thing I know, this man walked into my room and started grabbing things out of my closet and yelling that I was going to leave that night. "You are going to get out of this house right now! You aren't going to disrespect your mother!" he said, like he lived there too. He walked in and out of my room, taking things out of my closet: my shoes, my shirts, my jackets, my jeans, angrily setting them outside on the back porch. At that moment, I felt like a failure because I had decided to drop out of school, and on top of that, I felt like I was being thrown away while being seventeen and having nowhere to go. I was enraged and felt like I was not even good enough to have someone help me make sense of what I was experiencing inside emotionally. If you understand how trauma works, you know it can push you into an emotionally unhealthy place where nothing else matters. I continued to argue with them but eventually agreed to leave.

When I left my mother's house, I owned a 1981 baby blue box Chevy that I bought from one of my close friends, Atif Shaw. His parents, Mr. and Mrs. Shaw, had always been supportive of me as I tried to navigate my younger years, and he sold my mother and me the car when I turned seventeen so I could get around. This car was now all I had, so I took two trash bags filled with my belongings and shoved them in the trunk. I was in tears and told my mother and that gentleman that I did not want to be alive anymore. I was so full of rage, confusion, and hopelessness. Education was the last thing on my mind.

After tossing the last bag in the trunk, I sat behind the steering wheel and placed my head in my hands and cried and screamed. I then slowly started the car and made my way to the nearest gas station. It was late at night, and I was out of money and barely had any gas in the car.

I knew I had to reach out to someone, and so I stood in front of the gas station and did something I thought I would never do: beg for change to use the pay phone because I did not have cell-phone in high school until I was close to graduating. People walked in and out of the gas station, and I noticed people barely looking at me as I said, "Sir/Ma'am/Sir, do you have any extra change I could have?"

Standing in front of that store was humbling. Each person walked in and out, and still I stood there full of shame, asking for spare change. Imagine the trauma of standing there, having just placed all your clothes in the trunk of your car, and then having total strangers look at you like you were nothing or walk past you, treating you like you were invisible simply for asking for change.

Eventually a gentleman stopped and asked, "What are you doing out here so late? Shouldn't you be getting ready for school?"

I cut him off and asked if he had some change. He walked into the store and when he came out, he saw me again and tossed two quarters in my direction. I caught one quarter, and the other fell to the ground. As he walked off, he smirked and said, "I hope that helps." His reaction toward me did not help but made me feel worse. I grabbed the quarter off the ground and walked over to the pay phone.

MY FRIEND'S HOME

I had one person I felt like I could call in that moment: my friend from school, Erik Moore. I knew he had a good family. We would hang out from time to time, and I always saw his father, Mr. Moore, eat dinner with the family. His mother and sister were wonderful people. I guess I wanted to reach out to him because his dad would always say that if I needed anyone to talk to I could reach out to them.

Erik answered, "Hello."

"E," I asked. "Do you think your parents will allow me to come over and get some food?" I could hear the hesitation in his voice because it was a school night. He put down the phone. I could hear his footsteps running across the floor. Erik came back and said seven words I will never forget. "Come on over. My family loves you."

I don't even remember the two-mile drive, but it felt long. I thought about many things, mainly about home. Is home supposed to be this way? I needed to understand.

I drove up to Erik's house, and there was his father walking toward me holding a hot dog in one hand and a soccer ball in the other. My car window was down, and as I came to a stop, he got really close. Sticking his hand inside the window, he tapped me on the chest. "Look at me," he said. "You are a leader."

As I ate the hot dog, he handed me the soccer ball and said, "You are just like this soccer ball. This soccer ball didn't ask to be between two teams, and it doesn't have a choice which field it plays on. And, just like us, we don't get to pick where we are placed, who our parents are, or what environment we end up in. And, just like this soccer ball, you have been kicked around."

He continued, "But you are a leader. Sometimes life deals you a hand where you are kicked around. Do you want to know how this soccer ball survives all the kicks it encounters? It survives because of what's on the inside of it. There is something special inside you that the manufacturer has placed there. This soccer ball also survives the kicks." He turned the ball around. "What does it say?"

"Made for All Purpose," I read aloud.

"You have a purpose, and don't you ever forget it. Sometimes the kicks will hurt you, but you must not ever forget that you have a purpose. This soccer ball also survives because it has a goal. If you are going to overcome, you are going to have to set some goals that far exceed your environment, and never turn back, no matter what."

This man was not my father, but he modeled a sense of home that I had not experienced, and for some reason, I listened. He was one of the first men I could talk to at length and in depth. He used his own pain to relate to mine, teaching me what home truly means and the value of community. He spoke to me about overcoming life's challenges. He told me that he could relate to going through struggles because of poverty and that he was going to be there for me. When I think back on that conversation, it was the moment I knew I needed to make the decision to try and do something beyond what I had experienced.

A conversation like this was worth more than I could ask for in that moment and one that I had not really gotten or was able to receive up until this point. My mother had tried to get a few people to talk to me, but I felt none showed any real concern like Mr. Moore. Mr. Moore wasn't an educator: he was a family man, a community leader, a pastor, a man who loved his family, and someone who understood my struggle.

EXPERIENCING HOMELESSNESS IN HIGH SCHOOL

When considering education for those of high school age, the challenge is not merely academic but also deeply personal and existential. Whether enrolled or not, focusing on education becomes secondary when you cannot envision yourself as someone capable of even completing what is required. The turbulent circumstances that can disrupt the life of a child or teenager during their K–12 years can be profound and far reaching. Throw trauma, poverty, and social injustice in the middle of it all, and it creates a long spiraling road downward. The event that I am describing is one of many happening all around the country, and the prevalence of homelessness among high school students creating barriers to education is a very real thing.

Approximately 8 percent of high schoolers report experiencing homelessness.[1] This statistic not only underscores the critical nexus between stable housing and educational success but also hints at the insidious nature of how trauma and poverty can derail attendance and hinder academic performance and mental well-being. Living on the streets while trying to finish school—or even experiencing a brief period of being out of the house—is an unbearable experience filled with deep isolation. It leaves you feeling completely invisible. The feeling of instability that comes with homelessness has an enormous impact, psychologically and physiologically, on those experiencing it.[2]

The goal of educators being trauma informed is not to transform them into therapists or counselors but to equip them with tools and perspectives that create supportive and effective learning environments. It is about building awareness—awareness of how trauma affects students, shapes classroom dynamics, and influences teaching practices. By meeting students where they are, educators can cultivate spaces that promote both emotional well-being and academic success. According to data from the National Child Traumatic Stress Network, fully half of school-age homeless children experience anxiety, depression, or withdrawal compared to 18 percent of nonhomeless children.[3]

And that's where I was. I had sunk into a deep depression and was hanging by a thread in the margins of society and wrestling with the thought of being on the streets. As nights and days went on, the tension in my mother's home created more distance between us. I struggled to go back, often spending nights in parks near Campbellton Road, at a friend's house—like the Shaws'—or with my grandparents, Jessica and Herman Lester Sr. During this season, my father and others began to notice me spiraling. They understood that, given what I was carrying inside, I was struggling to find where home was and what it truly meant for me. As a result, I found myself moving from place to place.

Then one day, I had driven to the park—to just sit and think—where I often went to gather my thoughts or shed more tears. And in the park I said to myself, "I am not going to be a failure in life." I yelled that out loud at least ten times, in my car, at the top of my lungs. It was the moment when I decided that I was going to somehow finish school. I did not know how, but I was determined that I would finish for myself regardless of what anyone thought.

YOU WILL FINISH HIGH SCHOOL

Seeking a way forward, I went to the computer lab at the YMCA in the neighborhood to research how to get a GED. But I realized that I did not want to go that route after having a conversation with a man in his late seventies. He asked me what I was doing at the YMCA in the middle of the day, and I told him I was there to find out how I could finish my GED. Before I could go on about dropping out of high school and living out of my car from time to time, he cut me off.

"You will finish high school and get your diploma," he said. "Do not get your GED. You are better than this." He spoke with a pride-filled tone that moved me—and it was during a time when stigma and the GED were a real thing in the Black community and in society. There was almost a shame that came along with those three letters. Looking back, I believe it more than likely came from his lived experiences during the Jim Crow era. He followed up, "Me and your ancestors fought too hard for you to settle."

He spoke to me about the history of the GED, which was created as a path for veterans to obtain their high school degree—but only White veterans. When he was in the military, he told me, he wasn't permitted to take the test because the benefits of the 1940s didn't necessarily benefit Black soldiers like him. He explained how Black soldiers were often denied educational opportunities, access to housing loans, and adequate health care, along with other benefits afforded to their White counterparts.

In the aftermath of World War I, a protest by veterans in 1932 eventually led to legislative changes that culminated in the passage of the GI Bill in 1944, during World War II (1939–1945).

The GI Bill offered a range of benefits, including educational opportunities, housing loans, unemployment assistance, and business and farm loans, in recognition of the sacrifices made by those who served.[4] The creation of the GED coincided with this era of heightened attention to veterans' rights and benefits. Introduced in 1942, it was designed for World War II servicemen who had not completed high school. It served as an alternative certification to a high school diploma, enabling returning soldiers to pursue higher education or enter the workforce with formal qualifications.

This initiative was part of a broader effort to facilitate the reintegration of veterans into civilian life and acknowledge their contributions to the nation. However, the inclusivity of these benefits was not uniform. The racial inequalities prevalent in society at the time influenced the implementation of these programs, often sidelining the Black community and failing to fully address the needs of Black veterans returning from war. Local Veterans' Affairs offices often refused to approve loans for education and housing in predominantly Black neighborhoods. The GED, too, was not originally intended for Black people. Systemic racism prevented Black veterans from accessing this opportunity to complete their high school education.

A light bulb went off in my head. Originally, the GED had been a tool of discrimination, limiting the opportunities of Black veterans relative to White ones. Eventually, the GED was opened to Black people—but as soon as this happened, society began to devalue it, making the GED itself the tool of discrimination.

This conversation was transformative for me. Of course, obtaining a GED is a significant accomplishment and provides many people with opportunities they might not have had otherwise, and I do not have anything against it personally. But I saw that through the lens of the 1980s and 1990s, if you were a Black person with a

GED, you were somehow seen as "less than," and employers would view you through the same lens. The societal narratives that paint Black communities in a negative light add to this stigma. The GED is seen as a second chance or last resort, reinforcing negative stereotypes rather than acknowledging the socioeconomic complexities that influence educational paths. The impact of policies during the Nixon and Reagan administrations further compounded these challenges, limiting access to traditional educational pathways and pushing many Black people toward the GED, thereby perpetuating the stigma associated with it.[5]

I just did not want to go that route. I now remembered how adamant my mother had been about not getting a GED. I remembered that both she and my great-aunt had told me that it would be hard to land a good job if I decided to get a GED because of the stigma Black people were already dealing with for employment. The stigma was pervasive, as the GED was seen as a less than legitimate alternative, which could reinforce negative stereotypes and limit job opportunities. Armed with this information, I vowed not to take that path.[6]

A FIFTH-YEAR SENIOR

After reflecting on this and spending time away from my mother's home, my mother and I were able to talk through our misunderstandings. Because of her love as a mother, she allowed me to come back home, and I asked her if she would help me return to school. My mother agreed and did everything she could to reach out to the school to see if it was still possible. The principal gave me special permission to return as a fifth-year senior. This marked the beginning of a new chapter in my academic journey, although I knew I would have to endure the embarrassment of students younger than I was questioning why I was there. Without my mother, I do not think I would have ever finished high school. And, while she did show me *tough love*, she never stopped believing that I had what it took to graduate and become more than the examples I had around me.

My mother carried the weight of raising two children while holding on to the unshakable belief that education could be a way out for me. Even in the face of struggle, she modeled resilience, showing me through her own life that perseverance in education was not just an abstract idea but a lived experience. There were days when we didn't see eye to eye, moments when our communication broke down, but even then, she never stopped telling me to go to school. Even when I was too numb to listen, too caught up in my own battles, she kept speaking those words over me. And though I didn't always receive them at the time, those seeds took root.

Looking back, I now see how much strength it took for her to keep pushing me forward, even when I resisted.

My mother, Dr. Connie Walker, and me after she helped me get back into school as a fifth-year senior and encouraged me to finish high school.

She wasn't just fighting for me to graduate—she was fighting against the cycle that had trapped so many before me. She knew what was at stake, and she refused to let me become another statistic. And while we had our share of disruptions, her example gave me the courage to continue. I watched her work multiple jobs while raising two children alone, and I saw her push herself to finish not just one but two master's degrees, all while carrying the weight of single parenthood. She never had the luxury of ease, but she had determination. That determination became my blueprint.

Because of her, my sister Ashley went on to become an established educator with a master's degree, and I grew into a leader, using my journey to create change for others. My mother's unwavering belief in the power of education was why I finished. She not only fought for me to get back into school, but she also instilled in me the resilience to see it through. I am a reflection of her strength, and the sacrifices she made were not in vain. She showed me that no matter how far I got off track, there was always a way back—and that education wasn't just about earning a diploma but about reclaiming my future.

At my lowest moments, I found small, unexpected sources of inspiration and guidance because, yes, it takes a community to help break through the chains of injustice. It was the veteran, it was my friends' fathers, Mr. Moore and Mr. Shaw, it was the person experiencing homelessness who spoke hope into my heart, and it was my mother who continued to show me grace and believe that I could do it even after our misunderstandings. These people, from every walk of life, all helped me discover the strength and determination I had in myself to see my education dreams through to the end. Their unexpected belief in me when I had none in myself allowed me to grow a desire to pursue my education against the odds. This journey did not happen without internal battles and external judgments because, even after I got back in school and found a way to finish high school, I still struggled in my relationships with my family, my Black identity in relation to how Black people were viewed in society, and lingering trauma that formed more barriers for me before college.

These ongoing struggles I had and that others may face as they navigate similar choices should cause us to reflect on how much it takes to choose to move forward despite social and personal challenges. The road to healing and self-discovery is continuous, and resilience is born through the power of community support, which I found essential, even if that community is small. That's why I believe it is crucial to have nonjudgmental people in our lives who look past the circumstances and see the potential—offering the support needed to keep pushing forward. And I thank my mother for being that support, the one who said, "Keep on going . . . because education is what will help you soar."

A MOMENT OF REFLECTION

Navigating feelings of isolation, wrestling with depression, and lacking a stable place to call home make the traditional path to higher education extremely difficult. The psychological context of these struggles adds layers of complexity to the journey, and being aware of these challenges is essential to understanding how they impact educational trajectories. I would like you to imagine being a child or high school–age person faced with homelessness coupled with the heavy reality of leaving high school without a diploma. Picture the uncertainty of not having a consistent place to sleep, the strain of family conflicts, and the overwhelming fear of what the future might hold. Consider the emotional resilience required to confront each day with a deep yearning for a stable home, while trying to find a way back to education in the face of these types of struggles. Can you relate? Is this your story too? Is this the story of someone you have known or know now?

Reflect on the transformative power of a sincere conversation, a gesture of kindness, or the steadfast support of someone who sees the potential in the person in the middle of their despair. Think about the potential for family repair or how creating safe spaces that feel like home can ignite hope in someone on the verge of giving up.

As you ponder these scenarios, think about the many children, high school–age youth, or young adults who face these challenges daily, those whose stories capture the experiences shared in this chapter, striving to secure their place in a world that often overlooks them. Consider what it means to offer genuine empathy, understanding, and real support with trauma-informed care and concern to those quietly enduring struggles around them.

Ask yourself what role you can play in dismantling social oppression and obstacles and establishing safe spaces that nurture the potential in each person. This is an invitation to deepen your empathy and commitment to find ways in which you can initiate action in order to create pathways of empowerment and progress, especially for those who are navigating their journey against unfavorable odds.

SIX

FIFTH-YEAR PERSISTER

When the class I was supposed to graduate with was preparing to walk across the stage, I knew I wouldn't be able to walk with them. I had fallen too far behind and stopped going to school. Despite this, I still had many friends in the class and decided to attend the graduation ceremony. I sat in the back of the auditorium, embarrassed but also secretly hoping they would call my name. But they never did.

When I decided to go back as a fifth-year senior, the first day back to high school was not like the typical first day after summer break when a student is excited to show off their clothes, reconnect with friends, dream about the social clubs they will join, and plan out their senior year. Returning as a fifth-year senior added another layer of complexity. While navigating the academic demands, I was also trying to navigate the social dynamics of being a student who should have graduated the year before. When I walked back into the building, I was met with lots of weird stares as well as questions from educators who had probably thought I was locked up in jail or headed down a path of self-inflicted destruction.

"I thought you graduated," one person said.
"How are you a fifth-year senior?" another asked.
"So, you are going to walk twice?" asked yet another.

Students were mean, but none meaner than the teachers and educators who gossiped about my being back and the lack of confidence many had that I would be able to complete an extra year. One teacher pulled me aside on the very first day of school and told me, "You know, teachers are not really excited about you being back at school, but if I were you, I would prove them all wrong."

I was still burdened with so much trauma from my childhood, my environment, and watching my mother struggle as a single parent. I felt like I didn't measure up or have the inspiration to connect with my lessons in school because I did not have a safe space to process all the emotional pain. It all was a weight, and it broke me because I felt like it was too much for me to carry alone. It was a lot to carry for a growing, young Black man, and it is a lot for a community of people to carry when they find themselves being buried underneath the weight of systemic oppression.[1]

On my first day back, I was quickly ushered by administrators into the counseling offices to get my class schedule and to talk to the registrar about exactly how far behind I was and what classes I needed to graduate. After receiving my course schedule, I discovered that I was an entire year behind. But this extra year as a fifth-year senior would be just what I needed. To graduate, I would have to pass every class. Knowing there was no room for error placed even more pressure on me.

While the coming year would test every fiber of my being, I understood that this battle was about more than just proving others wrong. It was now deeply personal. I had made a commitment to myself to rewrite my own narrative and transform the pain that I had gone through into steppingstones toward my own journey of overcoming my previous educational decline. I'm still unsure how I prepared my mind for this, but navigating it was hard. It's challenging to avoid becoming another Black male statistic who could end up in prison or drop out of high school permanently. I was fighting a lot of battles, not just educational ones.

The 1980s and 1990s were an era in which Black students were cruelly and mercilessly labeled as foregone failures and dangers to society. They were villainized as "crack babies," "thugs," and "superpredators."[2] They were punished under a political system that disadvantaged them and created punitive language around Black education, especially in urban settings such as Campbellton Road. As a young Black man trying to beat the social statistics and finish high school, I was constantly questioning myself. Am I a thug? Am I destined for failure? Am I a lost cause, just another example of this "superpredator" social construct? I grappled with the societal labels and expectations placed on me, the misunderstanding from my peers on my return to school, and the judgment of some White educators.

Things at home were still not good, either. One month into starting back as a fifth-year senior, I had another disagreement with my mother and decided to leave the house again. I found myself back on the streets, with my belongings packed in the trunk of my car. This time, I was determined that no matter where I ended up, I would not stop going to school. I remembered Mr. Moore assuring me that one day I would overcome my environment and personal struggles.

While I was moving from place to place with my car as my only stability, I decided to reach out to my good friend Jeremy. Jeremy was one of my closest friends in high school, along with Octavious, Elliot, JB, Mario, and Trey. We all grew up in the Ben Hill community, and each of us had our own stories of struggle and finding our own way. Jeremy, Elliot, Trey, and I were the youngest in the group, a couple of years behind the others. Jeremy, Elliott, and I hung closer, shared our family pain and struggles, and related to one another through the social pain we experienced. None of us were able to fully connect to our lessons in high school, but we all stayed close because we saw ourselves going through the same struggles together as young Black men.

We also found ourselves at the alternative school together, and we used to meet up before school and talk about how hard it was to stay motivated. Educators seemed to show even less attention to students in that setting. In fact, they were with me when I encountered that man experiencing homelessness after deciding to walk away from school. Shortly after that, both Jeremy and Elliot were able to get into a boot camp program and finish school on time. After committing themselves to the process, they eventually ended up in the Air Force. Unfortunately, I had already dropped out of school and was not able to go through that program, but when Jeremy and Elliott were finishing training, that's when I was becoming a fifth-year senior.

After Jeremy graduated, he returned home for a short time before heading to the Air Force. He saw how I was struggling, living from place to place whenever my mother and I had disagreements. That's when I asked if his mom would be okay if I came to live with them. I told him to let his mother, whom we all used to call Cynt (short for Cynthia), know that I wanted more than anything to finish school. I asked Jeremy if he would be willing to talk to his mother, knowing that she was aware of the trouble we used to get into together.

To my surprise, she allowed me to stay—living in the family's large room in the front of the house, which used to be a garage. I felt a deep since of shame and brokenness inside, and I was without resources. There were days when I did not have lunch money or was unable to fill the car with gas. But every single morning I had to go to school, Jeremy, fresh off his night shift, would do something that would get me through the day. He'd literally be generous and fill up my beat-up Chevy with gas to make sure I had a ride. He would reach into his pockets and literally give me lunch money. He stayed proximate to my pain and suffering even as he wrestled with his own. "You gotta do this shit for you," he told me on the days when I wanted to give up, "and you got to keep pushing. This is for you, and because we got to go through all this shit, you got to decide for yourself. You've got to finish school for you!"

While Jeremy's care and generosity offered me a glimmer of hope in the world outside school, I was lucky to find some inside the school as well. Among the classes I needed to take to graduate was geometry. Geometry was taught to tenth graders at the school, and I recall the humiliation I felt walking into the class. But when I entered the classroom, the teacher, Ms. West, greeted me with excitement. She was a young Black educator in her first year of teaching. I was not used to teachers being excited to see me, so I didn't respond with much enthusiasm.

After class, she pulled me aside and asked me what was wrong. I opened up and told her about home. I told her about being a fifth-year senior, my fear of failure, and about the pain that I carried. To my surprise, she responded, "I am here to support you through this entire process and believe that you can make it. I can help tutor you and support you in any way. You are young, Black, and brilliant." I broke down in tears.

After that, Ms. West's classroom became a sanctuary for me. Her class gave me the confidence to attend and commit to the rest of my classes. I believe it was because she *saw* me (all of me). She was one of the first educators who had ever called me both Black and brilliant! Ms. West's support was life changing for me, especially at a time when I was feeling so isolated. Amid the unkind chatter about my return to school, her understanding and display of empathy became the encouragement I needed to persist.

Ms. West embodied what I now think of as *educational proximity*—the intentional closeness and engagement some educators have with their students' lived experiences, creating a deeper understanding of their needs, challenges, and strengths to cultivate meaningful and inclusive learning environments. Her proximity and awareness of my social location and trauma made all the difference. Ms. West became one of the first educators to motivate and encourage me during one of the most difficult years of my academic journey.

EDUCATIONAL PROXIMITY

Going back to school is immensely challenging. I know that firsthand. It is even harder to stay the course within a society that is primed to see the worst in you and within a community that is unable to provide the support you need to help you navigate both social and internal poverty. Trauma, stress, and the weight of societal and personal challenges can affect academic resilience and increase the likelihood of giving up in school. The trauma itself impacts students' ability to focus and show up with their full selves.[3] If you are Black and deal with extra societal pressures, you feel these stresses even more.

Proximity, however, can change everything. Proximity with the right, stable people and relationships and the right resources can significantly impact someone's ability to break the cycle of educational poverty and grow personally in a way that could set them up to finish school. A US Department of Housing and Urban Development study from 2011 looked at the effects of community and its impact on residents who live in areas of concentrated poverty. It examined how neighborhoods with higher concentrations of poverty can produce communal deprivation among residents, ultimately leading to negative outcomes for people.[4] The report concludes that collective efficacy—the idea that when people in a neighborhood come together and form strong networks, they can support each other and counteract the harmful effects of living in poverty-concentrated areas—can help improve communities facing poverty. Yet the report fails to address how growing up in this environment creates a lack of community, where the members are unable to sustain each other while being impacted by trauma and poverty because they themselves are experiencing it. This can create a deeper sense of hopelessness, where a person isn't able to see their efforts making a change right away.

I remember one time before I started back at school, standing on the corner with a few of my friends on Campbellton Road—friends who were also on the verge of dropping out. They didn't know how to make it out because there were no role models in their homes, and they had no clue how to even start back at school—neither did I. But somehow, with my mother's advocacy and the welcome of a friend's parent, I found my way back. We had community, but we did not always have guidance. For us and those like us, poverty and lack of access to a supportive community threatened to create perpetual cycles of deprivation. A more stable community of people is needed to stand in solidarity with those facing poverty to support them as they rise from the maze of injustice in their environment—and not just economically.

Millions of students are growing up in environments where the complexities of their struggles are significant barriers to their academic success. Could this be a form of educational injustice? These students often lack support from stable relationships, whether from educators or community members. They lack someone who was willing to stand with them long enough to help them navigate the hurdles in their life and school. Stable and close relationships are crucial for students from challenging backgrounds, as they provide essential support. This support can take various forms, such as mentorship, counseling and therapy, emotional encouragement, academic assistance, and a safe space for sharing thoughts and processing emotions. These connections help students overcome adversity and provide much-needed guidance and resources for breaking through systemic barriers.

When discussing education, it is important to understand that creating pathways to academic success involves more than just providing resources in the form of academic programs. It requires building relationships that can offer encouragement, solidarity, and wisdom, and that bring out the best in students, even when their environments suggest this is statistically impossible. Change starts with everyone realizing the importance of altering the trajectory for those who face barriers to educational progress. It starts with the wealth of relational equity that is grounded in being aware of the social traumas that a student, community, or group might carry. By recognizing that transformation can come from relational support, we understand that by lending our support, we will not only help students complete their education but also empower them to pursue higher education and greater opportunities. This investment in stable, proximate relationships is essential for breaking the cycle of poverty and ensuring that all students have the chance to succeed.

The table Poverty and Proximity lays out the challenges that poverty creates and the type of community support needed to navigate through them. Understanding these challenges reveals the critical need for community support to help individuals navigate and overcome the adverse conditions created by poverty.

Proximity is more than support. It embodies presence, awareness, and closeness in ways that surface-level support fails to include. When you support someone, it doesn't necessarily require you to know them. I have seen people offer support to others as a kind gesture or perform charitable acts of altruism. Proximity, though, is a deeper commitment. True proximity is where change happens because it asks the question of *how* we can show up in the world around us and allows our empathy and compassion to express themselves through service.

POVERTY AND PROXIMITY

Crime—Living in high-crime areas means people often lack the safety and security needed to focus on their goals or school.

Economic challenges—Poverty can hinder access to essential resources such as education, health care, and healthy food, reducing opportunities for upward mobility or educational success.

Health problems—Communities experiencing poverty face more health issues due to inadequate health care access and living conditions that could also impact educational outcomes.

Food deserts—Unequal distribution of food resources and lack of access to fresh, healthy foods lead to poor nutrition and related health problems. In Title I schools, this means that students might miss essential meals, leaving them hungry and making it incredibly difficult to focus in class and learn, which could impact overall health and educational outcomes.

Academic challenges—Underfunded schools in impoverished areas make it harder for students to succeed academically or sustain interest in the work long term, which ultimately contributes to educational injustice.

Family challenges—High levels of stress, disconnection, family conflict, and instability in families reduce their ability to provide support and guidance in making decisions regarding students' school.

Mental health challenges—Stress and trauma associated with poverty can impact mental health, leading to issues like depression and anxiety that could impact educational stability.

Urban hassles, environmental hazards—Living in an impoverished area often means people are exposed to environmental dangers, such as polluted air and water, toxic waste sites, and inadequate sanitation, which can also impact health, happiness, and prosperity. These hazards can lead to long-term health issues and exacerbate the cycle of poverty, a lack of mental clarity, affecting the overall well-being of those trying to succeed, especially in educational settings where good health is foundational.

Transportation barriers—Access to reliable transportation restricts opportunities for people to reach employment, health care, and educational resources. In fact, transportation is essential when thinking about upward mobility and progress. When public transportation options are sparse or unreliable, it makes attending school and work difficult, contributing to educational injustice and limiting socioeconomic mobility.

Limited access to technology—In the digital age, technology access is essential for educational success. In many low-income areas, however, there is limited or no access to high-speed internet or digital devices, creating a digital divide that leaves people unable to fully participate in education and employment, reinforcing educational injustice and inequity—as it relates to the digital divide.

Underfunded public services—Public services like libraries, recreation centers, and community programs are often underfunded in impoverished areas, leaving people without safe spaces to learn, grow, or connect. This lack of resources can stifle educational growth and personal development, further contributing to educational injustice.

Inadequate housing conditions—Housing in urban centers often suffers from neglect, with issues like mold, poor insulation, and a lack of proper heating or cooling. These conditions can impact health, making it challenging for people, particularly students, to focus on their studies and perform well, reinforcing the barriers of educational injustice.

Employment instability—In urban centers, people often have fewer job opportunities, which are frequently limited to low-wage or part-time positions without stability. This lack of a living wage often creates economic hardship that directly impacts a family's ability to support educational goals for their children, and students may need to work to contribute to household income, often sacrificing their education in the process.

Lack of political representation—Communities are often underrepresented in political decision-making processes, resulting in fewer resources and attention. Additionally, meetings about public interests are often held when people are at work. This systemic neglect perpetuates injustice and can create more educational injustice, as schools and services in these areas receive less funding, creating yet another barrier to equitable education and community development.

Lack of support and the need for stable, proximate relationships—
Now consider whether this is the environment where people around you are suffering and do not have the capacity to support you in a way that can help you get ahead because they, too, are suffering from the effects of poverty. When support is scarce, it can lead to a lack of guidance, connection, and meaningful relationships—essential elements that help people navigate challenges and find strength within their community. Support from a strong and connected community is essential for navigating these challenges. Being in proximity to people who can offer guidance, resources, and emotional support can positively shape a person's path, creating opportunities for growth and resilience despite systemic barriers.

Jeremy and educators like Ms. West embodied proximity. Jeremy wasn't just a friend; he was a lifeline when I was drowning in a sea of emotions—abandonment, systemic injustice, and the pain of social, material, emotional, and spiritual poverty. He didn't have to say much some days, but his actions stuck with me. He showed me that sometimes home isn't a place, it's the people who refuse to let you fade into the background, the ones who see you when you feel invisible. Jeremy's front room became more than just a place to sleep; it was where I found a bit of the stability amid the chaos and summoned the courage to go to school each day. This stability helped me to focus on my studies. Those at school had absolutely no clue that as a fifth-year senior, I was striving to finish school while staying in a friend's home for a couple of months—made possible by the generosity of a peer and his single-parent mother.

Encountering proximity in these crucial, vulnerable moments shaped my approach to community leadership. Today, I strive to embody proximity as an ethic, a language, and a practice. This practice has taught me that to truly serve, we must be willing to share not just our resources but also our lives with those we seek to walk with, especially when people are suffering in ways that are hard to articulate. It's in this type of proximity we get to see our humanity wrapped up in other people's humanity, becoming what Dr. Martin Luther King Jr. called "interconnected."[5]

THE COURAGE TO PERSIST

I finished my fifth year of high school. I committed and applied myself. I did it all with the systemic, institutional, and interpersonal challenges of racism and poverty hanging over my head. I became a successful "fifth-year persister"—a term that honors the determination of these students to complete their education despite the obstacles.[6]

Let me be the first to tell you that it was not easy. I was fortunate to find a few people who stepped in and supported me through one of the hardest years of my academic career, which became the foundation that set me up to achieve further education. There was my mother, who advocated initially for me to get back into school, even when I took her through an up-and-down battle from the trauma that I was carrying. And because she fought for me to go back to school even during our rifts, I was able to finish my education.

There was Ms. West, who was both my educator and a champion for my success.

After my graduation ceremony, West Lake High School, June 2001.

Then Principal Marc Jones and another teacher, Ms. Royster, saw my efforts and joined in with Ms. West to encourage me toward success as I showed up every single day to learn. There were educators like Mr. Muhammad, a substitute teacher back then who's now a psychologist. He pulled me aside one day after substituting in a class I was taking, telling me that I had a gift of writing and speaking that became the seed that has continued to grow and blossom to this day. There were also the resource officers, Randal Ponder and Officer Driver, who saw my resilience and consistency and helped me because they knew that I needed attention as a young Black man trying to navigate all that I was experiencing.

I am not sure if all these people knew about the challenging outcomes for those who try to come back for an additional year after not graduating on time, but it was that village that fueled my resilience in finishing school, even with all the pain and trauma that I was carrying inside. And in June 2001, because of their support, I graduated from West Lake High School with my college preparatory diploma—a milestone moment in my life that I will never forget.

A MOMENT OF REFLECTION

I know for a fact that if it was not for a small group of socially aware people who decided to be proximate with me and push me, I could have easily fallen through the cracks. It was very difficult to articulate how much support I needed to avoid giving up on life and on myself, even before considering education. This support was crucial in helping me navigate these challenges and move forward.

Reflect for a moment on the intertwining of proximity and education in the narratives and statistics you've encountered. Have you ever considered a lens of race with trauma, the weight of fifth-year persisters, and how often these accounts go beyond mere academic performance to contemplate the lived experiences of students navigating such hardships? Think about the daily hurdles and systemic obstacles that students from socially marginalized communities face not just in their pursuit of education but also in their very presence in the learning environment.

Now consider the historical backdrop and the ways it continues to shape educational access and equity, alongside the realities of poverty for those still struggling. Have your thoughts on educational disparities recognized this deep-seated history, or have they only focused on the immediate challenges of the present?

Reflect on the barriers and systemic injustices that students from historically marginalized communities navigate not only within their educational journeys but also as part of a broader historical continuum. How do these enduring marks mold their perspectives on learning, their aspirations for the future, and their resilience in the face of daunting odds? How do they mold your perspective?

Think about the power of recognizing our shared history in the fight for educational equity. Imagine the change we can create by working together to address and heal from past and present injustices. Picture a future where every student, no matter their background, has the same opportunities to learn, grow, and succeed. By building close, proximate relationships within our communities, we can provide the necessary guidance and resources to overcome barriers and create real, lasting change.

SEVEN

WHEN FAITH CONFRONTS TRAUMA

ap tap tap.

The music was blaring, so no one could hear the police tapping on the window of the apartment. I was sitting on the sofa in the middle of a party at Gordon State College, and no one was cognizant enough to pay attention. The taps got louder, and the police officers figured out the window was open. They lifted it up, stuck a gun through the window, and said loudly, "Turn down the music and open the door now!"

The police were there not because someone phoned in about a loud noise violation but because they had viewed footage that contained my image taking alcohol from a local store to supply this party. I was popular on campus at the time so I was quickly identified. They were there to arrest me.

When the officers walked in, they ignored everything going on in the apartment that was illegal and asked, "Where is Terence Lester? We do not want anyone but Terence Lester."

I sat there, scared out of my mind while everyone looked in my direction. I was identified, placed in handcuffs, and the officers walked out and placed me in the back seat of their vehicle.

There was a crowd now standing around the police car, and it seemed like everything was happening in slow motion. I immediately thought of all the times people would say to me that someday I would end up in jail.

It takes a lot of work to rewrite narratives like,

"You are going to be just like the brothers from your community who became statistics."

"You are going to be dead or locked up in jail one day."

"Your future doesn't look too bright because of how you are."

I realized how many times these lines had replayed in my mind, over and over.

All the other college students watched me get dragged away, like a scene from movie. It was *this* moment, with all of its pain, that would be the beginning of a life-changing journey.

We arrived at the jail. They booked me and traded my clothes for an orange jumpsuit. I thought my whole life, at that moment, was over.

But a random encounter in the jail cell would cause me to wake up and finally commit myself to being the best I could be.

I need to pause here to say that I am not advocating for any young person trying to fight their way through trauma and pain to experience what I experienced. Rather, I suggest that sometimes conversations that we need to have, in order to wake us up, come from people from whom we least expect them.

I wasn't there twenty minutes before they placed me in a cell with about sixteen other inmates. The town was small, so they placed many inmates in one large cell. There was a mixture of people there who had committed more serious crimes than I had. Some were in there for assault, others for more violent crimes like attempted murder, and others for armed robbery and carjacking.

I had just turned twenty. I was scared, not just for my life but also for my future. Was this my reality? Poverty, trauma, and minimal guidance, just trying to find my way forward while making wrong decisions?

Initially after high school, I had enrolled in Atlanta Area Technical College. There I struggled to find a concentration or path, and I didn't receive the guidance I needed from instructors or counselors. Feeling lost and unsupported, I eventually dropped out. About a year later, I felt the urge to try school again. I thought maybe if I moved away from Atlanta, I could focus more, and that is when I found Gordon State, a small college in Barnesville, Georgia, about an hour and fifteen minutes from Atlanta.

I enrolled there but had no real path or direction. No one had ever really sat me down and talked about a path after high school. Many of the relationships that helped me navigate high school were gone, and my environment did not prepare me to have a plan for higher education or how to navigate it as a first-generation Black male college student, all while carrying the lingering trauma and pain from not really feeling like I had any family support.

About an hour after I was placed in the holding cell, I noticed an older inmate walking over to me. He asked me a question that I will never forget:

"What on earth are you doing in here?"

He wasn't asking what I did to get in there. He was asking because he saw I was young, and he wanted to know why I was in there wasting my life. This question hit me harder than I expected. It was like he saw right through me. But even greater than that, he asked the question because he had been locked up for years, and he was concerned I was ruining my life.

It was like he saw a part of me that even I didn't fully understand. His straightforwardness stirred something deep inside me that created a sense of urgency to change the direction of my life, even though I couldn't quite grasp how to do it just yet.

Afterward, he asked me if I was going to eat my dinner. I could not even think about food at that moment, so I gave him my dinner while I wondered what was going to happen to my life.

A young Black man, just a little older than myself, who came in after I had, also randomly started a conversation with me. He said, "I am probably going to be in here for a while because I can't reach my parents."

I asked him why, because I knew his pain.

He responded, "They are overseas preaching."

"Preaching what?" I asked

"Preaching about God," he said.

I laughed it off, but he was serious. He explained that he was in there because he did not have his license when he was stopped by the police because he had left his wallet at home. That's when the conversation took a turn. He started talking to me about faith and how my life had purpose and that God loved me. His words made me think deeply and seriously about my life. I will never forget his words: "I know you have gone through a lot, and I can see the pain in your eyes, but one day God is going to use your life because it has more meaning than what you think."

How could God love someone like me—given my past, the challenges I had faced, the injustice, the difficulties, the wrong decisions I made, the weight of poverty and trauma, and everything I was carrying while trying to navigate an educational path? But the sincerity in his voice and his story about having a pastor for a father were unsettling yet comforting. I really did not understand what faith was, and sometimes I questioned that if God was real, why would he allow all the suffering we see in the world? Especially the suffering I saw in my own family and community.

But his words stayed with me because I could not understand for the life of me why, at that moment, he would be there with me for something as simple as not having a driver's license. Maybe there were racial implications because he said that he was pulled over for something he did not do—not putting on a turn signal. This small town was known for discrimination toward young

Black men. But all I knew was that in that cell, this young man who was a little older than me spoke to me about faith and about my life having a greater purpose—at a critical moment when I needed guidance. Thinking about that moment and the pain I felt, even now I still get chills. Until that point, outside Mr. Moore, no one had really taken the time to talk to me about my worth and value and what that meant from a divine perspective.

But his words, which I wasn't sure I was ready to hear, resonated with me on a level I couldn't ignore. I guess I needed to hear a message that cut through the nihilism that communities suffer when they are unable to make sense of the meaning of life because of poverty, pain, and oppression.

My mother was contacted and drove all the way down to Barnesville, Georgia, to plead with the store owner to drop the charges. Before I knew it, a couple of hours had passed by, and the young man and I were still talking. Just before my mother arrived, he asked if he could pray for me. When my mother arrived at the jail, she told me that if I were to get out, I would most likely have to leave the college. It had to be around three in the morning, and I believe I said my second prayer ever—second only to the first prayer I said in the car at the park when I was eighteen. I simply said, alongside this young man, "God, if you allow me to get out of this, I will change my life and never look back." In that moment of prayer, everything felt both heavy and light: the weight of my past and the possibility of a brighter future.

Can you imagine having a moment like this where you are in trouble, stuck in a jail cell with all those inmates in a small town with a racist history? My prayer was a simple plea, yet it felt like the most significant promise I had ever made to myself. I wasn't sure the prayer would work, but the next day was a huge indication that something different had taken place.

A SECOND CHANCE

The next morning, I was escorted to the court and seated next to my mother. When I walked in, I noticed a large room filled with mostly young Black men and a few White men who were older waiting to be sentenced. A jury, comprised of mostly White jurors with a few Black people, was seated along with a small crowd that was taking up the wooden, pew-like seats and reminded me of an old Baptist church layout—only this was a courtroom. There was an older Black couple sitting next to my mother and me, and the wife leaned over and whispered to us that this judge didn't "play." He was known in the community for giving harsh sentences to young Black men, and it was for this reason she was there. She wanted to see what was going to happen to her son.

While not trying to excuse the reason I was there or avoid responsibility for what I had done, I did remember reading once that Black men were disproportionately sentenced in comparison to their White counterparts for similar crimes, a statistic I now took personally. Recent studies corroborate this, showing that Black defendants are often subjected to harsher sentences, which is a stark indication of the systemic racism still prevalent in our legal institutions today.[1]

This pattern of racial injustice in sentencing is not just an isolated issue. Broader policies, such as the War on Drugs, created a school-to-prison pipeline that has disproportionately targeted Black communities since the 1980s. This policy has significantly increased the incarceration rates for Black men, particularly for nonviolent drug offenses.[2] The impact of these policies continues to resonate deeply, affecting not just people but entire communities, contributing to a cycle of poverty and limited educational opportunities as outlined in the poverty and social conditions layer of the Generational Trauma and Educational Inequity Framework.

Research by M. Marit Rehavi and Sonja B. Starr further high-lights the depth of this issue, indicating that judicial discretion, often influenced by racial bias, contributes to these sentencing disparities, with Black men receiving sentences approximately 10 percent longer compared to White offenders who are convicted of similar crimes.[3] And once a Black man is incarcerated, his chance of finishing any type of higher education drops even lower. These odds are illustrated in the Generational Trauma and Educational Inequity Framework table that appears in the introduction to this book. These were the odds that I was facing.

One by one, the judge called people to the front of the courtroom, asked whether they had representation, went through the details of their case in front of everyone, and then pronounced their jail time. Not probation, jail time. I was sitting there, nervous but also preparing myself to face my fate. Each person was called up individually for their various violations and then had to endure the embarrassment of the judge's stern and belittling tone as he passed down their sentences. In fact, the young man called up before me did get actual jail time, which made me more afraid that my own sentence would be similar to his. As I sat there, sur-rounded by faces as anxious as mine, I couldn't help but wonder how much of our fate was sealed by our actions, by the color of our skin, and by the expectations and prejudices that awaited us long before we ever set foot in a courtroom.

When the judge finally called my name, I stood up. He read the charges, then noted the support and plea of my mother trying to raise me and my sister as a single parent—and that the owner of the store had dropped the charges. He then paused. He looked at my mother, as if he could see her history, our pain, and trauma, and said words I will never forget.

"I do not know why I am doing this, but I am looking at your mother, and I can tell there is something there. She has probably had to be tough with you and do the best she could. And today is your only second chance. I am going to dismiss this case, and if you end up in here again, I will give you time."

Perhaps within the judge's pause, there lay a moment of empathy expressed within the confines of a flawed system. But in that moment, something shifted within me. I felt a change begin to take place, moving me away from a person who had to endure suffering to someone determined to overcome challenges and take control of his own destiny.

I told myself that when I moved back home, this time I was going to commit to changing myself. Whatever that was going to look like, I was determined to become more than everything I had gone through.

As I walked out of the courtroom, the sound of the judge's gavel still ringing, I knew my journey was not just about personal redemption but about the second chance I needed to change my life completely.

I didn't know if God had done this, but I silently thanked God. I walked out of the courthouse and headed to the apartment where I was staying, packed up my car, withdrew from school, and headed back to Atlanta, all in that same day. I didn't know why I had been given another chance, but I had. Even though I had withdrawn from college a second time, I was committed to finding my path and continuing my education.

Little did I know the Black church would be what God used in my own life, similar to the lives of my ancestors who were discriminated against, to help me find communities healing from trauma and, ultimately, to become the person God always intended for me to become.

THE IMPACT OF THE BLACK CHURCH

The Black church has always been at the forefront of supporting the civil rights movement. In fact, the Black church is where

Black people have gone for safety, to be seen and affirmed as leaders, and to organize resistance against hatred. It has also been a place to cultivate the faith that has given the Black community its strength to fight against all that has been against them. These communities have also been considered educational centers in order to come against racist policies and tactics that have been used to keep Black people from learning. And as we examine our current societal moment, it appears history is beginning to repeat itself. School systems in several states, including Texas, Florida, Missouri, Utah, South Carolina, North Dakota, Michigan, Virginia, Tennessee, and others, are challenging and banning books—among them, Dr. Jemar Tisby's book *The Color of Compromise*, a mere mention of which led to the firing of a professor at a Christian University;[4] *Born a Crime: Stories from a South African Childhood* by Trevor Noah; *The Bluest Eye* and *Beloved* by Toni Morrison; *The Hate U Give* by Angie Thomas; *The Color Purple* by Alice Walker; *The Black Friend: On Being a Better White Person* by Frederick Joseph; *The 1619 Project: A New Origin Story* by Nikole Hannah Jones; and *And Still I Rise: Black America Since MLK* by Henry Louis Gates—that contain essential information about Black history.[5] This kind of systemic suppression links directly to what Supad Kumar Ghose argues is trauma inflicted by historical and ongoing educational injustices against Black communities.[6]

I know this because, when I was younger, my grandmother Jessica Lester (my dad's mother) attended the historic Wheat Street Baptist Church. I visited the church with her when I was a child. She was my first introduction to any type of faith, and she talked with me about what the pastor and the church were doing to combat the racial ills that were plaguing the community. At the time, when I went to church with my grandmother, I really didn't understand what was being preached. I only attended because I loved my grandmother. I later learned that she took me to church with her a lot when I was a young boy when my father was in jail for a little over a year.

We didn't attend church regularly, but I went briefly with my mother on Easter when I was a young child. And while I didn't have much contact with the church, I believe the small but consistent exposure from my grandmother gave me some spiritual foundation. I also remember being baptized at Wheat Street and having her drag me around the church telling her peers that I would one day be a preacher—a grandmother's intuitive prophecy that would someday be fulfilled.

Years later, I learned that faith communities for Black people helped to cultivate what Dr. Jemar Tisby calls the Spirit of Justice when our very existence was threatened.[7] The Black church was pivotal, not only offering spiritual safety and rest but also functioning as a "movement church" during the civil rights movement, deeply intertwining spiritual formation with social justice efforts.[8] The Black church was also responsible for helping to start historically Black colleges and universities (HBCUs) when Black people were not given access to educational opportunities beyond grade school and competing in the workforce. The role of the Black church in the Black community was central to educational access for many people. It functioned not only as a spiritual sanctuary but also as a center for political and educational activism. Reflecting on these childhood visits, I now see how it laid a foundational layer in my understanding of the Black church's historic role as both sanctuary and battleground. It was probably the seed that began to germinate inside me as I exited that courtroom.

The Black church served as the epicenter for the civil rights movement, providing a space where strategies were planned and voices could be safely raised against systemic oppression. Many denominations were instrumental in the establishment of some of the earliest Black colleges and universities in the United States, serving both as sponsors and as venues for education when no other options were available. These institutions were founded in the late nineteenth century, a time when legal segregation denied Black people access to higher education as a result of the lack of educational equity and equal opportunities. Churches like the African Methodist Episcopal Church and the Baptist Church played crucial roles in founding and funding schools like Wilberforce University[9] and Morehouse College,[10] which remain prominent educational institutions today.[11] Schools like Morris Brown, where several notable Black scholars emerged (like James Alan McPherson and Carrie Thomas Jordan, pioneers of Black intellect), were first founded in communities where faith and education converged to resist evil, hatred, and social exclusion.[12]

I guess it was important to my grandmother to take me to church when I was a child because she was born in 1932 and witnessed segregation firsthand. She faced being unable to travel to certain parts of town, endured seeing the colored water fountains, witnessed Black people experiencing violence, and attended underfunded schools. Additionally, she had to comply with segregated seating in buses, was restricted from entering certain restaurants and theaters, and lived through the constant threat of racially motivated attacks. When I was growing up, my grandmother and her peers understood the profound significance of the Black church for those facing oppression. Although I did not stay involved in church because of my experiences growing up, I later realized that my grandmother's influence and the seeds she planted during my initial exposure to the Black church would eventually take root and draw me back.

ONE SMALL YES

Two days after I moved back home, a friend of mine, Harvey Strickland, asked whether I wanted to go to church. I told him I would go.

I said I would because I had just moved back to Atlanta and wanted to be around positive people so I could cope with the feeling of failure that I had after having to drop out of another school. He told me that he was dating a girl who went to the church and had been attending ever since. I decided to attend the small group they were having for men.

When we arrived, there was a pastor and a small group of other guys in this Bible-study group. I was a little hesitant because I had experienced some really horrible things as a child with people from communities of faith. However, this night I was a little more open than normal. Surprisingly, the warm and welcoming atmosphere that night began to soften my hardened perceptions, offering a glimpse of what a true community feels like. Surrounded by faces that spoke of similar struggles and shared hopes, I felt a sense of belonging that I hadn't realized was missing from my life.

As the discussion progressed, the pastor shared stories of the church's engagement with the local community, from advocating for young Black men to providing support for those impacted by systemic failures. This demonstration of the church's commitment to its community members resonated deeply with me, creating a sense of belonging and showing me a practical example of unconditional love in action. It wasn't just about spiritual teachings; it was about active engagement and support that addressed the real and pressing needs of its members. Here was a community that not only preached love but also practiced it in tangible ways that directly affected the lives around the community where the church was located.

I do not know why, but this pastor spoke in a way that made faith seem real and active beyond personal salvation. While sitting there, with his worn and tattered Bible, the pastor spoke about God's love in a way that suggested that it was powerful enough to restore a person who had gone through struggle, suffering, and things that were related to injustice. He shared this one verse that I will never forget. This verse spoke to me of an unconditional love I had never experienced, a love that did not wait for me to have my trauma together, my family perfectly intact, my pain resolved, my educational journey flawlessly planned. It reached out amid all my suffering and failures. It was a radical idea that contrasted with the conditional acceptance I had often felt in my life and within my own family.

He said, "But God demonstrates his own love for us in this: While we were still sinners, Christ died for us" (Romans 5:8).

This pastor talked about how God's love in the person and work of Jesus showed up regardless of our social location, trauma, poverty, or having been wronged by others in the face of injustice. God's love wasn't defined by that but is powerful enough to give us the safety, comfort, and forgiveness needed to be liberated, restored, and repaired. This message of unconditional love struck a chord within me, that I was worthy of love and acceptance regardless of my past failures or even how I was viewed in society.

I guess that night when I listened to that pastor, I heard my mother's pain and cries for me to go a different path and my grandmother Gloria's voice from when I was a child. I didn't know what to expect coming to the church, but apparently, I just needed to know that I was loved without any prerequisites.

I couldn't help but draw the connection between my own journey and the larger tapestry of systemic inequality and barriers that felt like traps set to catch people who came from where I came from.

It was a moment of clarity, one that caused me to remember that young man in the jail cell who caused me to see my story as part of a collective struggle for love, dignity, and justice. Because I had gone through everything I had been through—homelessness, a gang, failure in school, a fifth-year-senior experience, trauma, a lack of guidance, and wanting to one day complete a doctoral degree—I asked the pastor in that moment how I could receive the love that he was speaking of. He led me in prayer and confession, and I accepted a relationship with that brown-skinned Palestinian Jew named Jesus. In that prayer, I felt an empowerment wash over me, a clear call to shed the weight of my previous life and step into a new identity defined by strength and faith. It marked the beginning of my journey not just toward personal healing but toward becoming a proactive agent for change in my own community.

It was a small yes that gave me the hope I needed to know my life was worth more than what I had gone through. Although I did not become a member of that specific church, something changed in me that night. I believe that experience was real and just as divine as a person, who was just passing through, sharing his faith with me in a small, country jail cell.

As I left the church that night, a new resolve took root inside me. I now felt that God was with me and that I could start again, with love covering me and walking with me in solidarity. It was the church that gave me the community I needed to heal and overcome some of my challenges. Imagine if every church became a space of healing and restoration, where a community of people could walk with those who have experienced trauma, homelessness, and social suffering. Imagine if these communities surrounded people with the support they needed to find the courage to overcome the injustices of this world. Imagine if every church could reclaim the power of being an organism that helps those plagued by poverty—they could provide the support necessary for people to pursue higher education.

It was in the church where I entered into relationships that changed the trajectory of my personal and educational life. It helped me connect with mentors and counselors, provided spaces to attend men's groups and youth ministry, and gave me opportunities to serve and stand with others in the community. It exposed me to books that shaped my spiritual foundation, provided wisdom and guidance, and deepened my hunger for scholarship and reading across various fields of study.

It was also the church where I began to discover my voice, sold my first self-published book, and performed spoken word in front of the entire congregation—marking the beginning of my journey in using art as a means of healing and self-expression. This community and its people—many of them people of faith who believed that God's power and love were greater than the injustice, trauma, and suffering of this world—helped to get me where I am today.

A MOMENT OF REFLECTION

I believe divinity and grace met me at a pivotal moment in my life when everything I had fought to overcome during high school could have led me down a path that has ruined many young men's lives. However, it was in the sacred space of the church where I found a safe haven to explore the theological concept that God is always on the side of the oppressed, as the late Dr. James Cone explained in his liberatory theology. Do you have these personal experiences? If not, consider the experiences within your community, especially in relation to the roles that the Black church or sacred faith spaces played in being safe spaces and educational centers. Consider how these institutions have not only been sanctuaries against systemic oppression but also pivotal spaces for learning and empowerment in the name of the Lord. How have these spaces influenced your understanding of social justice, community support, and personal growth?

If they have not given you these insights, how has that harmed your understanding of the world and those who are marginalized? Contemplate the historical significance of the Black church in providing spiritual guidance as well as acting as a crucial educational resource during times when Black people were systematically denied access to mainstream educational opportunities. How does this dual role of the church resonate with your experiences or those around you? Additionally, think about the church as a whole and how it could become a trauma-informed space that offers hope and healing beyond the salvation of the soul. How can churches today extend their role to support those emerging from poverty, providing not only spiritual solace but also practical support in continuing education and overcoming systemic barriers?

Reflect on the potential of faith communities to act as catalysts for change, offering hope in Jesus and tangible support systems that empower individuals to pursue educational and personal development goals. This moment of reflection is an invitation to appreciate the multifaceted roles that faith institutions can play in providing the type of support that helps to build resilience, hope, and educational advancement. It's also a call to consider how these spaces can be nurtured to better serve as communal support for those facing the intersecting challenges of poverty, trauma, and systemic exclusion.

EIGHT

WORK AND WORTHINESS

After my life-changing experience in church, one of my first jobs after moving back to Atlanta was in a small warehouse. There were only two workers: me, responsible for shipping the packages, taping boxes, and other tasks; and my supervisor.

It wasn't a busy warehouse, but for some reason, I had to stay in the back, where it was hot, while my supervisor remained in the front with the air conditioner. I was looked on as just the help, apparently not worthy of the benefit of staying cool. My supervisor, a young White man, would frequently remind me of my race and make condescending and sarcastic remarks to let me know that he thought Black people were inferior. He would often start discussions with me about Black poverty or Black crime and make racialized comments about the breakdown of the Black family. He would also quote conservative commentators while discussing the low college attendance rates among Black people, and he often went out of his way to remind me that I did not have a college education and that I was a Black worker and inferior to him.

I never asked to be a part of these conversations and wondered what caused him to start them with me. Maybe he thought he was secretly tearing me down with his rhetoric and comments, but this actually was causing something to grow in me: a deep sense of determination to become more than what I had experienced in my life up until this point.

One morning, I arrived at the warehouse, and it seemed like he had a chip on his shoulder. Whenever he was in that kind of mood, I became a punching bag for racial comments and remarks. On those days, he would stand outside and chain-smoke. The appearance of the office space and the smell of those cigarettes are forever etched in my mind. It was 2004, and the warehouse had brown commercial-grade carpeting, desks from the 1990s, a small bathroom, and a couple of nondescript pictures hanging randomly on the walls. In the back, there was a small open warehouse space of about 3,500 square feet where I would work, drive the forklift, and ship packages from the warehouse shelving.

That morning when I arrived at work, he stared at me and, even before greeting me or saying, "Good morning" said, "I got a question for you . . . do you think many Black men your age work mediocre jobs or go to college?" The comment offended me deeply. This man seemed to want to take out his frustrations on me by saying something so offensive without knowing me as a person or my dreams, or even what I had been through. But this morning, he questioned my worthiness itself.

Grounded in the faith I realized I had and began to develop while being in the Black Church, I learned that my worth was not defined by systems, racialized comments, or injustice but by the truth that God had given it to me. When I read the words of 2 Corinthians 5:17, which say that God has the power to make all things new and that I could be a new creation, I believed it and wanted to honor myself through the lens of how God saw me, not how I was seen because of being Black or even because of what I had journeyed through.

I decided to speak up for my twenty-one-year-old self and responded, "I don't know about anyone else, but I do know that growing up the way I did was tough. However, I plan to grow once I figure out my path toward one day earning a PhD. I would like to someday use my story to help people that have suffered and struggled the same way I have by being a community leader or speaker." Talking like this made me remember what Mr. Moore had told me, and I wanted my humanity to be acknowledged. It also made me remember what my father told me while playing sports, "Always lean into your voice and lead."

His response was unforgettable. He laughed at me. His laughter was so discouraging for me because he was saying that he didn't believe I was worthy of college. There were even times that he would plainly say, "You'd be better off sticking with being a forklift driver or a warehouse worker." But my courage in speaking up for myself had empowered me. From then on, each day at work, I did my job to the best of my ability and, during down moments, researched on the computer how to obtain a doctorate. I also practiced poetry, lining up the boxes and speaking to them like they were my audience. It was this space where I nurtured my passion for education, writing, and speaking.

WORDS SHAPE THE FUTURE

My supervisor's demeaning words targeted four areas historically tied to an ideology rooted in white supremacy. This type of ideology always seeks to undermine and belittle Black and Brown people in a way that would attempt to erase their humanity, intellect, and existence. These attempts to undermine are rooted in what I call The Four Pillars of Erasure: Voice, Visibility, Value, and Vision. Each of these four areas interlock with one another and are foundational to one's physiological and psychological sense of humanity. Consider how, when these four areas are suppressed, it can cause additional barriers for someone like me or others from starting higher education or returning to it after a failure or later in life.

Understanding the power of words is crucial when considering education. When you're navigating a world that appears designed

THE FOUR PILLARS OF ERASURE

Voice: *What you have to say*—Historically, there has always been an attack on the voices of those who spoke up about oppression and the injustices done to Black people, similar to the resistance faced by leaders such as Martin Luther King Jr. and Malcolm X during the civil rights movement. Their experiences with government surveillance and misinformation campaigns like COINTELPRO were used to target and discredit their voices.[1] Voice is crucial; it's connected to a person's humanity through their ability to communicate their truth to the world. When voice is silenced, it hinders people from expressing the essence of who they are as humans and as children of God.

Visibility: *How your presence is included*—The lack of visibility of those who are oppressed was historically designed through public policy, violence, and other exclusionary measures. This took the form of redlining, requirements for people to enter through back doors of restaurants, and restrictions on which drinking fountain "colored people" were allowed drink from. These drinking fountains were this country's first form of hostile architecture.[2] This particular era of discrimination reflected a broader societal attempt to deny the visibility of Black people. To be seen and heard is an essential part of who we are as human beings; to be unseen is a form of dehumanization. The Harlem Renaissance challenged these attempts to erase Black voices and visibility, as Black people showcased their dignity through expressions of culture, making our presence and intellect visible while asserting our worthiness of the same spaces as anyone else.

Value: *How your worth is measured*—When a person's voice and visibility are threatened, their inherent value is also threatened. This

---

[1]Virgie Hoban, "'Discredit, Disrupt, and Destroy': FBI Records Acquired by the Library Reveal Violent Surveillance of Black Leaders, Civil Rights Organizations," University of California, Berkeley Library, January 18, 2021, www.lib.berkeley.edu/about/news/fbi.

[2]Terence Lester, "Belonging as an Act of Justice," *From Streets to Scholarship* by Terence Lester (Substack), April 16, 2023, https://imterencelester.substack.com/p/belonging-as-an-act-of-justice.

is problematic because people must fight internal battles about whether they are worthy or not. If a person is to be silenced and publicly sanitized, then are they worth anything? An example of this is when Black people were devalued by being considered only three-fifths of a person.[3] However, the abolitionist movement challenged these ideas, advocating for the ending of the enslavement of Black lives and confronting laws and social norms that treated Black people as property.[4]

Vision: *What you think and contribute*—Vision is last because when your voice, visibility, and value are threatened, it causes a person to struggle to try and see how their vision and dreams are able to survive within a context of oppression, where all you're hearing is how your dreams and vision are not worthy, accepted, or able to belong. Consider the Black Panther Party's initiatives where community health programs and children's breakfasts demonstrated a powerful response to systemic suppression. This helped in nurturing a vision of improved health and well-being for Black communities in resistance to white supremacy.[5] However, this vision was torn apart by the power and racial hatred of public officials who targeted the Black leaders, aiming to keep the Black community oppressed.

---

[3]Patrick Rael, "A Compact for the Good of America: Slavery and the Three-Fifths Compromise," Black Perspectives, December 19, 2016, www.aaihs.org/a-compact-for-the-good-of-america-slavery-and-the-three-fifths-compromise/.
[4]History.com editors, "Abolitionist Movement," History.com, October 27, 2009, updated March 29, 2023, www.history.com/topics/black-history/abolitionist-movement.
[5]"Black Panther Party: Challenging Police and Promoting Social Change," National Museum of African American History and Culture, accessed June 21, 2024, https://nmaahc.si.edu/explore/stories/black-panther-party-challenging-police-and-promoting-social-change.

to limit your upward mobility, especially in accessing higher education or striving to transcend the obstacles stacked against you, believing in the possibility becomes much harder. Historically, this sentiment hasn't always been explicitly stated as de jure discrimination, as much of the racism has become de facto. It has manifested in other ways, with power structures hindering marginalized groups from accessing the resources and support needed to break free from systemic injustice, such as voter suppression laws, redlining, underfunded schools, biased standardized testing, employment barriers, lack of affordable housing, and a lack of access to mental health support and health care.

My supervisor's words replay in my head to this day—not because they control me but because I am grateful that I did not allow them to define my future. I am more than his words and the way he treated me. I think about the countless other people who have battled against similar insults by society because of stigma. These words do not define who I am now, but they do remind me of the long struggle Black people have endured since arriving on the shores of the Americas.

Why did his words fail to define me? Because he did not know my history. He did not know Black people's collective struggle and their effect, or what I had to overcome to be working at that warehouse. He made sure I knew that his college education was paid for by his wealthy family, and that he was set up for success and I was not. Which explained why he enjoyed taking shots at my family and Black culture. Being in that type of space, with a person who doesn't think much of you, your actions and words say a lot.

Despite my past challenges, I was determined to find a way back into school to finish what I had started. But if I am being honest, there were elements from his remarks that stung because he was critiquing a lived reality that was not his own. My community *did* face concentrated poverty, I personally did not have many role models who had gone to college, and there were families who were split apart because of mass incarceration deliberately targeting our community.

However, my supervisor's understanding lacked the necessary historical context of systemic injustice that has shaped these conditions—partly, I believe, because he hadn't worn my shoes or spent any real time getting to know people from a different social location than his, with different world experiences. He was unaware of the impact of the collective suffering and historical trauma of Black people and how his words contained immense harm.

Like many first-generation college students, and like many who work labor jobs in environments lacking opportunities, I faced significant odds—socially and systemically—in thinking I could go from a warehouse back to college. However, in reality, it did not matter whether I wanted to pursue higher education or whether he thought I was worthy of it. What mattered was my continued belief in myself and in my own worth and value. I believe that is why Dr. Martin Luther King Jr., in his speech "The Drum Major Instinct," emphasized the worth of each person regardless of their social location. King said,

> Everybody can be great, because everybody can serve.
> You don't have to have a college degree to serve.
> You don't have to have to make your subject and your verb
>   agree to serve.
> You don't have to know about Plato and Aristotle to serve.
> You don't have to know Einstein's theory of relativity to serve.
> You don't have to know the second theory of thermal
>   dynamics in physics to serve.
> You only need a heart full of grace,
> a soul generated by love.
> And you can be that servant.[1]

Dr. Martin Luther King Jr. connected the act of service and contribution to the inherent worthiness of every individual, irrespective of their background or social status. In "The Drum Major Instinct," he made it clear that greatness is not defined by academic achievements or societal positions but by the capacity to serve with a heart full of grace and love—an ethically grounded foundation that also fuels the courage to pursue education as a means of justice and transformation.

This emphasis underscores the radical democratization of worth, shifting the measure of greatness away from hierarchical or material standards and rooting it instead in the universal accessibility of service, which affirms dignity and purpose for all people regardless of their origin or status.

RESEARCHING SCHOOLS AND HISTORY

Before my dream could turn into a reality, I had to explore the history of what it took for my ancestors to reach a space where our resilience and collective strength played a role in overcoming barriers both past and present. This understanding gave me the inspiration I needed as I continued to grow in my faith in God and resist the social stigmas placed on young men like me. Through my research, I discovered that access to higher education, employment, and other spaces where representation mattered had always been a struggle.

It was at this point that I decided I would not let my circumstances or my supervisor's words determine my future. Each day, my passion to go back to school grew, perhaps fueled by this supervisor's mistreatment. However, being in a faith community helped me to realize that God had a purpose for my life that was somehow connected to a higher education. All I know is that it takes courage to get back up every time you get knocked down in life or navigate tragedy, systemic injustice, oppression, unexpected life events, personal failures, or falling short when you're trying to complete a goal. However, once that courage is found, taking another step forward becomes easier.

NONEQUITABLE ACCESS

Historically, terms like *equitable participation* and *affirmative action* were attempts to ensure that Black people and marginalized groups, who were usually excluded due to white supremacy and discrimination, were not barred from society, employment, educational opportunities, or fair wages. The first use of the phrase *affirmative action* came with President Kennedy's Executive Order 10925, signed on March 6, 1961. However, its origins trace back to the 1940s, with President Roosevelt's Executive Order 8802. This order sought to ensure "the full and equitable participation of all workers in defense industries, without discrimination." During the brief Kennedy era, Vice President Lyndon B. Johnson and Hobart Taylor Jr., a well-connected Black lawyer, expanded and crafted this policy to ensure equal treatment for all people regardless of race, creed, or origin. This policy began to gain momentum through social movements that fought for justice, equality, and equity, most notably during the civil rights movement of the 1950s and 1960s.[2] While these terms turned into public policy that evolved over time, their original intent was to provide representation for those excluded from opportunities.

In his second term, President Donald Trump signed executive orders that effectively dismantled affirmative action measures, notably revoking Executive Order 11246—a pivotal directive established in 1965 by President Lyndon B. Johnson to promote equal employment opportunities and prohibit discrimination by federal contractors. This has raised concerns about the potential erosion of voting rights protections, which could disproportionately impact historically marginalized communities.[3] This action feels like a deliberate attempt to turn back the clock on hard-fought progress, undoing decades of work to dismantle systemic barriers to participation.

In his inaugural address, President Trump emphasized his vision for a "colorblind and merit-based" society. While this rhetoric suggests equality, it has been criticized for overlooking the persistent structural inequities that affect historically marginalized communities.

However, in reality, this language ignores the structural inequities that persist and dismisses the unique challenges faced by historically marginalized communities.[4] It creates a false premise where racial identity is treated as irrelevant, when in truth, its social construction continues to dictate access, opportunity, and treatment in society.

These actions and narratives have raised concerns about a regression in civil rights advancements, echoing historical struggles for representation and equity. The dismantling of affirmative action policies and the promotion of a colorblind ideology risk undermining decades of progress aimed at addressing systemic barriers to participation.[5] This also undermines the sacrifice of those who gave their lives for this work.

It is important to consider the historical context of systemic efforts to deny Black people access and success, both economically and educationally, but also in other ways that would continue to uphold the erasure. In fact, the idea of equal opportunity and equitable access was not fully upheld initially because it was fought against in cases like *Regents of the University of California v. Bakke* and *Grutter v. Bollinger* and, through presidents like Reagan, was later banned in certain parts of the country.[6]

Understanding this context is crucial because it paints a picture of how universal access to higher education was historically met with discrimination. On June 29, 2023, the Supreme Court ruled 6–3 to strike down affirmative action practices in college admissions. According to the Brookings Institution, this decision marked a departure from the original intent of ensuring equal access to work and education and racial equity, especially for Black students striving to access higher education. Justice Ketanji Brown Jackson made a powerful dissent against this ruling, explaining how it was a setback against the barriers that were already in place for students who emerged from cities like Atlanta, where poverty and trauma were high due to systemic injustice. She stated that this decision "condemns our society to never escape the past that explains how and why race matters to the very concept of who 'merits' admission."[7]

A recent report, "Understanding Equity Gaps in College Graduation," reviewed data from all public and private nonprofit universities in Virginia and several in Connecticut (as these states provided detailed student data, and the results likely reflect national trends). They found that a common counterpoint to calculating graduation rates based solely on race and ethnicity is that Black and Latino students often face greater challenges in college than their peers who are not Black or Brown. These students generally have lower test scores and high school grades on entering college, making them more susceptible to academic struggles and dropping out. Additionally, Black and Latino students frequently deal with financial hardships that can force them to leave college for economic reasons.[8]

Affirmative action was supposed to rectify past injustices against Black people and marginalized communities by ensuring equal opportunities—specifically those in education—through public policy, as predominantly White schools were known to deny college applicants access when they discovered the student in question was Black. As the Brookings Institution reported:

> Previous state-level affirmative action bans have shown that race-neutral admissions policies are ineffective at improving racial equity in higher education. One study found an immediate 1.6-percentage-point decrease in Black enrollment in the most selective schools after such state-level bans. School leaders in some of these states filed amicus briefs to the Supreme Court in support of affirmative action, stating

that their schools' Black enrollment has dropped and remained lower than pre-ban levels after more than a decade.
And now, minority enrollment is predicted to decrease by as
much as 10% in highly selective colleges following the elimi-
nation of race-conscious admissions nationwide.[9]

Brookings further indicated, "Recently, HBCUs have been working
to correct those injustices. In 2021, Maryland paid $577 million
to the state's four HBCUs to settle a fifteen-year-old lawsuit
alleging a discriminatory funding system that favored traditionally white schools. A similar situation is currently unfolding
at Tennessee State University."[10]

This historical context reveals not only the challenges but also the
persistent exclusion of marginalized groups, especially Black people.
Brookings also reported that this was an opportunity for HBCUs to
create space for those seeking access to higher education and emphasized the importance of investing in historically Black colleges and
universities. These institutions have long served as havens for Black
students, providing them with the support and encouragement they
need to succeed. By allocating more resources to HBCUs, we can
mitigate the impact of this recent Supreme Court decision and
ensure that Black students still have access to quality education.

Even though I had a dream of one day obtaining a PhD, the path
was still littered with challenges and *educational injustice*. I started
finding articles about how hard it would be to obtain a degree without
financial or emotional support, and I did not know where to start. I
needed a miracle. So, I started praying for the right community of
people who could help me on my quest for a higher education.

FINDING HOPE IN COMMUNITY

While working in that warehouse, I began to attend a church in Atlanta that my mother introduced me to. My mother knew that I was

trying to change my life. She had started going to a church community and, not long after, invited me to visit, which helped to mend our relationship. In that nurturing community, not only did I feel I had found my voice, but Bishop Dale C. Bronner even helped me self-publish two books. One was a book of poetry titled *The Mind of Me*; the other was titled *U-Turn: The Teenage Turnaround*, an earlier book about how I changed my life, to which he wrote the foreword.

It was in this church, Word of Faith Family Worship Cathedral, where God began to change my life. I began to grow in discipleship and find my calling into the ministry. This community of faith provided the space I needed to heal, share, and talk through all the suffering I had endured even as I was discovering who God wanted me to become, given my story and history. It was here where God provided a place for me to connect with a diverse community of believers from various fields of work, including Black college graduates, doctors, lawyers, real estate investors, entertainers, small business owners, and musicians who overcame the odds stacked against our community. It was the exposure I needed to see beyond what I had experienced. Being in proximity to a lot of different types of successful people who I never would have had the chance to be around provided me with the exposure I needed to have my life transformed. These were people who, despite our collective historical traumatic backgrounds, had found ways to become who they were meant to be, with their faith at the center. I needed that, and I still tear up today when I think of how many people have not yet found that type of community.

This community was grounded in the good news that God restores, and it offered me a space to glean from the wisdom of the elders there. I learned about faith, Black history, and the importance of education. I learned a lot about life from the testimonies of those who were willing to share, while also wrestling with my own faith and the persistent realities of injustice and suffering in the world. God used this space to do as the text teaches: "I make all things new" (Revelation 21:5 NKJV). This community gave me the safe space to believe I could change and overcome the odds stacked against me. I was becoming a new person. Communities of faith, when functioning correctly and in a healthy way, can create a safe space where people can heal and not feel ashamed of their suffering. These spaces—where faith meets trauma, poverty, and injustice—are where theology becomes both personal and public.

A TRANSFORMATIVE RELATIONSHIP

One day, as I was walking down the church hallway, I ran into Mr. Eason.

Mr. Eason led the business institute, was a very successful real estate developer, and was well-known in the church. He was a passionate person with a contagious personality, who was known around the church for his spiritual wisdom and brilliance in business. I'm not sure why I decided to speak to him, but before I could, he spoke to me. He said that he had seen me perform poetry, speak to the youth in the church, and deliver speeches from the stage during the main service. He began talking to me about my future.

He said, "You could be a powerful leader and use your gift to change people's lives."

Honestly, I felt like a hypocrite because I knew I had dropped out of college and was now working in a warehouse where I was being treated unfairly. Before he finished his statement, I looked sorrowful, and that's when he asked me, "What's going on?"

I told him I would love to tell him my story one day, if he wouldn't mind. Later that week, he and Mrs. Eason invited me over to their home. I told them my entire story: where I grew up, my struggles, how I started writing, and how I wanted to go back to school.

He, too, shared his struggles and told me how he overcame them by becoming a wealthy real estate developer. When I mentioned school, he interrupted me and said, "If you decide to go back to school, my wife and I will be right there to support you." And they were true to their word.

I finally found a school to attend. It was a small Bible college because, at the time, I felt I had a strong calling toward being in the ministry.[11] Mr. Eason not only encouraged me to attend but also helped pay for my degree, supplementing the money I had already saved up from the warehouse job. I didn't ask him for help; I simply shared my story because I wanted someone to hear what I had journeyed through, and he stepped in to support me with resources to pursue my education.

Mr. and Mrs. Eason became an integral part of my personal community in the church. They encouraged me, mentored me and, down the road, paid for my eventual wedding to my wife, Cecilia. Mr. Eason even walked my wife down the aisle because her own father was in prison at that moment in our lives.

Their support set me up and became what I needed to build further community. This type of support would later give me the courage to not only finish my bachelor's degree but to go on and obtain two master's degrees—one in counseling, the other in theological studies. Both degrees set me up to do work in the school system as an educator, where I began serving middle-grade youth who were considered at risk.

Before I knew it, my life had changed. By the time I was twenty-eight years old, I had four degrees and had gone from an ex–high school dropout, ex–gang member, and ex–teenager experiencing brief moments of homelessness to being a youth pastor, a young adult pastor, and later a church planter. I later began doing community activism work, founding an organization called Love Beyond Walls, which I continue to lead today as a published author and speaker, traveling to advocate for those experiencing homelessness and poverty. God used community to encourage, rescue, and liberate me, and it literally changed the trajectory of my life. Before Mr. Eason passed away in 2023, he witnessed me starting a nonprofit organization, Love Beyond Walls, which would affect tens of thousands of unhoused people and educate thousands more on the importance of serving the community and seeing others through the lens of empathy.

He sent this text message to me almost a month before he passed away and made his transition: "Son, I am so proud of the leader, husband, and father you have become. Keep leading, leader!" I still get chills reading this text message because it was as if, somehow, he knew that the investment he made in me and in his community would help me to reach my potential. I believe he felt that seeing me overcome was his reward.

A CALL FOR SPACES OF SUPPORT

When we think about the countless people who are suffering from not having enough personal resources to start school or from a lack of community, it becomes essential just to hear someone say, "If you start, I or we will be there." It took a community, dedicated people investing time and resources, a safe space, faith, and God meeting me in my poverty and trauma to give me the courage to start again. It requires immense courage to rise after life knocks you down, especially when dealing with tragedies, systemic injustice, unexpected events, personal failures, or falling short of goals like finishing school. However, once that courage was found, I believed that taking another step forward was possible.

The church community in Atlanta became a sanctuary where I could heal, find my voice, and receive the encouragement I desperately needed. When we think about college access, we must consider these essential elements that could help people like me have the capacity to break free from the chains of systemic injustice.

NAVIGATING BARRIERS
A four-step approach to higher education

Step 1: *Personal resilience*—Finding the resilience and determination to persevere involves cultivating a belief in your own abilities that is supported by setting goals and accessing trauma-informed care.

Step 2: *Resource support*—Support in the form of monetary resources, grants, and other resources is crucial for students emerging from impoverished backgrounds.

Step 3: *Community*—Having access to a healthy supportive community is essential. This community can offer guidance, wisdom, and encouragement as well as help hold you accountable during the long educational journey.

Step 4: *Faith and spiritual support*—Having a set of core beliefs grounded in faith can provide inspiration and hope. This faith is often strengthened within a supportive community of believers. [1]

---

[1] This list is not exhaustive.

Community is more than just a group of people. It's a network of emotional, spiritual, and sometimes economic support. People like Mr. and Mrs. Eason and others in this faith community, who believed in my potential and supported my educational journey, were crucial in helping me transition from working in the back of a warehouse to finishing multiple degrees and becoming a community leader, advocate, author, and speaker.

The impact of community support cannot be underestimated. For some, this support may come from a community of faith; for others, it might come from a nonprofit organization, a local community gathering, or a program. This support can take various forms, but it is vital that we recognize the power of community and the impact it can have on people striving to overcome systemic injustice.

A MOMENT OF REFLECTION

Looking back, I can see a clear connection between the pivotal relationships that entered different stages of my life and where I am today. Whenever I lacked a clear pathway to higher education or personal growth beyond my social context, there was always a person, place, or community that helped me see beyond the limits I placed on my own potential. I honestly never thought some of those life-changing relationships would be found in the context of a community of faith. Consider the importance of safe spaces being trauma informed with the four R's and the four additional R's— spaces that are spiritually supportive—and how they could be resources of inspiration for people harmed by structural racism and erasure. These spaces would be intended to help people find the strength and courage to overcome systemic challenges. But we must ask ourselves, Why aren't more churches placing resistance to injustice, social awareness, and trauma-informed care at the center of their mission to serve the community? We need to consider how these spaces can be nurtured and expanded to better support those facing the intersecting challenges of poverty, trauma, and systemic exclusion. By doing so, churches can become more effective communal support systems that address the comprehensive needs of their members and the broader community.

Reflect on your personal journey and the experiences within your community. How have supportive networks influenced your educational and personal growth? How did you manage to get ahead in life, school, your career? Consider the ways these communities have provided emotional, spiritual, and practical support, helping you to overcome systemic challenges and pursue your dreams. Now, think about the people who haven't had that same access to support.

It's truly a collective mission to work together to create a network of support that provides not only spiritual safety for one to seek healing and peace but also practical assistance in continuing education and overcoming systemic barriers. This moment of reflection is an invitation to appreciate the multifaceted roles that healthy, supportive communities can play in building resilience, hope, and educational progress. It's also a call to consider how we can further develop these spaces to better serve and uplift those who need it most.

NINE

REDEMPTION AND THE HEALING POWER OF COMMUNITY

When the Tulsa Race Massacre occurred, Black Wall Street was not only destroyed by the hatred and violent acts of white supremacy but was also deeply impacted as a community by the trauma inflicted on its people. The Tulsa Historical Society and Museum provides a detailed historical account of the events leading to the Tulsa Race Massacre. On May 30, 1921, Dick Rowland, a young Black man, shared an elevator with Sarah Page, a White woman, in the Drexel Building in Tulsa. The following day, Tulsa police arrested Rowland after rumors about their encounter spread.[1] As a White lynch mob of two thousand gathered outside the jail holding Rowland, a small group of armed Black men arrived to oppose them, dressed in their World War I army fatigues. A confrontation ensued and a shot was fired.[2] The next day, the Greenwood District, a thriving self-sustained Black community, was set on fire by White rioters. Governor Robertson declared martial law and detained six thousand Black Tulsans at the convention hall and the fairgrounds.[3] The violence lasted for twenty-four hours, resulting in the destruction of thirty-five city blocks of Black businesses and homes, over eight hundred injuries, and an estimated death toll now believed to be as high as three hundred.[4]

In 2021, Viola Fletcher, a survivor of the Tulsa Massacre, gave public testimony before members of a House Judiciary subcommittee. Reflecting on that traumatic moment when she was only seven years old, she said:

> I still see Black men being shot, Black bodies lying in the street. I still smell smoke and see fire. I still see Black businesses being burned. I still hear airplanes flying overhead. I hear the screams. I have lived through the massacre every day. . . . I am 107 years old and have never seen justice. I pray that one day I will. I have been blessed with a long life—and have seen the best and worst of this country. I think about the terror inflicted upon Black people in this country every day.[5]

She was seven years old when it happened, and her mind was still sharp enough at this public hearing to recall her experiences in vivid detail. All remaining survivors spoke about how the community never recovered, and many of those who survived the attack still see, feel, and realize the stain and impact on their community as the decades have passed. In the same year, a report released by the National Bureau of Economic Research testified to the horrible pain and economic impact the massacre itself had on the community:

> The 1921 Tulsa Race Massacre resulted in the looting, burning, and leveling of 35 square blocks of a once-thriving Black neighborhood. Not only did this lead to severe economic loss, but the massacre also sent a warning to Black individuals across the country that similar events were possible in their communities. . . . For the Black population of Tulsa, in the two decades that followed, the massacre led to declines in home ownership and occupational status. Outside of Tulsa, we find that the massacre also reduced home ownership. These effects were strongest in communities that were more exposed to newspaper coverage of the

massacre or communities that, like Tulsa, had high levels of racial segregation.[6]

Nearly a century later, we can still see the damage and decay of this once-thriving community. In fact, Hughes Van Ellis, who was a hundred years old when he testified, told the subcommittee, "We were left with nothing. We were made refugees in our own country." Lessie Benningfield Randle had felt safe and happy in Tulsa before "everything changed."[7] Each of the witnesses spoke about how White violence burned down vibrant businesses and claimed the lives of innocent people. Bodies were discarded in the nearby river in the most dehumanizing way possible. Some survivors even said that the experience was so horrific that they could still see the dead bodies in their minds, nearly one hundred years later. These public testimonies were the living survivors' statements for a lawsuit that sought reparations for the damage and destruction left on the Greenwood community over a century before.[8]

If we were to open up a forum broadly where people could testify to their own, firsthand accounts of how they have been impacted by a long system of injustice or the personal ruins their lives have faced as a result, what would they say? Who would they be? And what type of impact would it have?

I think about families who would stand up to testify about their experiences with trauma or the ways that historical trauma has caused mothers to be separated from children, fathers to be disconnected from their children, and the economic, health, and social challenges. I think about the environmental racism—how this caused poor health in Black and Brown communities—and about the educational injustice. I believe we would hear stories from those who have had to endure harsh social living conditions that have made quality education inaccessible. These conditions have impacted generations of families, causing an inherent fear for those wanting to pursue education due to generational trauma and a lack of communal support.

I think about this in my own life when it comes to what I have journeyed through in my family: the breakdown, the trauma, the family disconnect, the challenges with education, and the emotional weight and pain. These experiences are deeply connected to historical events and generational trauma, and looking at this through the lens of education, I realize how heavy the generational trauma is and how much harm has been done, making it hard to find places of healing, forgiveness, and educational progress. The generational trauma from events like the Tulsa Massacre can be seen not just in historical records but lingering in the lived experiences of people and families today in that community. I realize that, as a Black man, this contributes to the way I grieve the collective trauma and suffering of my ancestors and what our community has had to journey through. But it also informs the way I show up and fight for healing and repair. Witnessing survivors speak up at that hearing gives me courage to share my own personal redemption and healing that happened within a faith community. It gives me courage to profess that by the grace of God, I experienced a moment of repair with my own father that I will never forget. This courage is found when looking at our collective history and seeing the strength of survivors who profess, "I am still here . . ."

When I reflect, I know this redemption is a testament to the healing power of the community that surrounded me during a time when I was seeking a life beyond all that I endured—emotionally, socially, and spiritually.

A LIFE-CHANGING PHONE CALL

In 2017, while sitting in a Love Beyond Walls meeting, I received several back-to-back phone calls from one of my older sisters, Tasha. When I didn't pick up, she sent a text message.

I read her text over and over again, hoping that it did not say what I had just read. I stepped out of the meeting and called my sister back.

"I just received a phone call that said Tyrone has just had a stroke, and it is not looking good," she said. "Tyrone was on the phone with one of his friends named Red, and Red believed that he was having a stroke right then."

Tyrone, my father, was being rushed to the emergency room at Grady Hospital, the very same hospital where I was born. I felt sick and couldn't catch my breath. My father and I had not spoken in over a year. Our family connection was in ruins. The news hurt me deeply.

On one hand, I was hurt that this was happening to my father, and I feared that he would pass away before he ever got a chance to know me and be proud of me, something every child longs for no matter their age. On the other hand, I had a lot of built-up pain from my childhood trauma that I was still working through. I was at a loss of knowing how to feel in that moment.

Questions flooded my mind: Will my father pass away before we ever get to repair our relationship? How do I show up for him? What do I do when the majority of our relationship has not been good with communication?

I honestly did not know what to do and felt emotionally frozen. While I continued to heal from my own social and personal trauma, this news added another layer that I was not prepared for. Words and clear thoughts escaped me when hearing this news.

When I received the news about my father, I had been leading Love Beyond Walls for about four years alongside Cecilia. I had been attending church for about a decade, developing my faith and serving a community of people who had been overlooked, as I had been.

I returned to the meeting and, without thinking, told everyone I would not be able to stay. I then walked outside to my car and began to sob. I sobbed because I did not want anything to happen to him, especially because at that moment our relationship wasn't the best. My hands trembled, and it took me a while to start the car. When I finally did, I just started to drive. I had no destination in mind, but I knew I could not be around people. Tears streamed down my face while I felt confusion, anger, disbelief, and fear. I had a moment with God in that car and asked, "Why has my life been so hard, and why is there so much distance and pain in my family?"

That's when I calmed down enough to call my wife. She answered the phone, and I shared the news with her. I asked her, "Cecilia, what should I do? I am afraid that my dad might pass away, and I do not know what to do."

I wasn't expecting her response.

She said, "God changed your life, gave you a chance to impact total strangers who are suffering from homelessness. You need to go and serve your father in exactly the same way you serve those who you don't even know through Love Beyond Walls. You need to show support in the same way the community showed you support and helped you to get where you needed to go. Be close."

Hearing those words brought such a calm to my heart. I knew she was right.

I turned the car around and headed straight to the hospital to be with my father in whatever way he needed me. However, I need you to know that that same little child who was afraid when I witnessed the violence in my home was the same frightened little child driving to be with my father in his time of need. But this was my father, and regardless of our past, I would want my son to be there for me, so that is exactly what I did. I showed up to support and serve my father, and I am grateful to God that I did.

I had developed a set of core values that included service and compassion, and I didn't want to deviate from them. I didn't want to just preach a message of proximity but to actually become the very community my father needed. I chose to live out one of the verses that I used to start our organization to serve my father: "For even the Son of Man did not come to be served, but to serve, and to give his life as a ransom for many" (Mark 10:45).

GETTING CLOSER TO MY FATHER

When I walked into the ICU, my father's body was paralyzed on the left side. He told me that the doctors had performed emergency brain surgery to break up a blood clot and attempted to remove it. Soon afterward, the doctor came into the room and told me that he believed my father would eventually regain his mobility.

During the time in the hospital, my younger sister Ashley and I sat with him, stayed overnight, and were just present with him as he continued to heal. That was tough, but as we talked briefly during my visits, I could tell this major health event was causing him to reflect on the fragility of life. There were even times when he would look at me, with tears in his eyes, and say, "T, I am so glad that you are here . . . thank you for being here . . . I am just glad I am alive to see you."

Days later, when he was about to be discharged, my dad asked whether I would help him get his medication, drive him home, and help support him while he recovered. My wife's encouragement to "just serve him too" inspired me to have the courage to serve him *willingly*. That would eventually lead to a divine moment that would turn out to be one of the greatest redemptive works outside my own personal journey of rebuilding my life.

A PHONE CALL A DAY

Weeks after my father left the hospital, he began to gain mobility on his left side. He would call me almost every day, and we would just talk about nothing in particular. Just communicating with one another can be used by God for restoration and redemption. It felt strange at first to talk that often because we had been in and out of each other's lives—not seeing each other as consistently as we had during Little League sports. Sometimes we spent more time together than others as I transitioned into young adulthood and eventually became a grown man. However, I could tell that something divine was happening in my father's heart, and in mine. He began to talk about how he was starting to believe that God had spared his life so we could repair our relationship.

These conversations gave my dad a chance to apologize and get to know me more than I had experienced when I was a child, and it gave me the space to forgive. There were times when he would talk about the historical discrimination his community faced, the drugs that ravaged his childhood community, and how he internalized those experiences from the trauma that was created in the environment where he grew up in Washington, DC. The trauma inflicted by white supremacy in the 1950s and 1960s created harsh living conditions that impacted him in numerous ways and caused his environment to experience ruin—emotionally, spiritually, economically, and the many other violent ways that poverty destroys the potential of community and the lives of people.

His words gave me perspective on just how dangerous the effects of systemic injustice and generational trauma can be and how it can be passed down through generations. Hearing about his experiences allowed me to understand the pervasive influence of historical oppression on our family. His stories allowed me to see his humanity and just how much our community had suffered. Even though some of our talks were accompanied by tears— much-needed tears—each and every conversation would end with an "I love you." Slowly, God began to repair our relationship.

OPEN TO COMMUNITY

I'll never forget a phone call I received one day from my dad. He asked about my work with Love Beyond Walls because he had been following what I was doing in the community and saw me on the news. When I explained how I was ensuring that people who were poor and unhoused had access to resources like showers, identification, healthy food, and community, he responded with, "That's good . . . I am proud of you." He then continued talking about how he was becoming more "grounded in the Lord" and starting to go to church. This was my father's own way of sharing with me that he had established a relationship with the Lord, as he would often say. My father would often talk about faith and say that throughout his life, the one thing he wished he would have embraced earlier was "groundedness" and faith in the Lord. He was now, he felt, becoming more grounded in the Lord.

A couple of months after his nearly life-ending stroke, my father asked if he could come to hear me preach whenever I was near where he lived. I was not only leading a nonprofit but also preaching from time to time in communities of faith, incorporating the love of God in my message as I spoke about oppression, justice, compassion, and never forgetting those who are marginalized. I told my father that I would be preaching in July of that year, 2017, at a church in West Georgia. He asked me if he could come hear me, and I agreed because our friendship had begun to grow. He arrived that morning to hear me preach for the first time in front of almost five thousand people.

With his permission, I told the story of what had happened to him and how his life was spared by a person he was on the phone with who suspected he was having a stroke. I also spoke about the doctor who performed the emergency surgery, who was not even supposed to be at the hospital that day. I continued sharing how I went to serve him and how that became a catalyst for repairing our relationship. I wanted to find a way to honor the relationship we were establishing, so I talked about the power of community and what it can mean to the people around us—whether we know them or they are our own family. After the service, my dad walked into the room where I was and gave me a big hug.

Me, my father, and my wife, Cecilia, after he heard me preach and speak for the first time, reflecting the trust and bond we were building.

Later that day, he called me and told me that I was his favorite preacher and speaker and that he wanted to get involved in our work at Love Beyond Walls. He started to tell me that he was proud of me every time we spoke, and I believed him. Our bond would continue to grow, after each time we talked, until my father become one of my best friends.

FORGIVENESS

It was 2017 when my dad called me at the beginning of December. He talked for a long time about life, forgiveness, and how he wanted to repair his relationships. He wanted to be different. He wanted to show up in the world as a person of faith and not as a person of rage. That's when he asked me, "Do you think you and your family would like to come and see me get baptized?"

"Baptized?" I said. I was shocked, even though my father had started to go to church after his stroke and gave his life to God and to the community of faith he was attending. I almost dropped the phone because I could not believe what I was hearing. But I immediately answered, "Of course! My family will be there to support you." So, on December 31, 2017, right before midnight, I got to see my father profess his faith in the Lord and be baptized. Afterward, I gave him a big hug.

Witnessing my father get baptized at Kingdom of God Ministries International was a moment etched deeply in my memory, one I will never forget.

Our relationship continued to grow over the next seven years, grounded in friendship, faith, and a love for food and sports. He would come over to my house, and we would go fishing together at a neighborhood pond with me and my son, TJ—connecting three generations. We spent hours by the water, casting our lines and talking about everything from our favorite sports teams to deeper life lessons, and he would burst out laughing each time TJ, who was not even ten yet, would throw his fishing line far in the water because he was amazed that he was so young but knew how to fish well. We played chess, laughed, and cooked together, creating cherished memories. During the first year of Covid-19, social distancing made it challenging to see each other often, especially as he was getting older. But we spoke on the phone almost every single day for hours.

CANCER

As the pandemic continued into its second year, we had less time together, but through our conversations, I got a chance to really know my father more before our world was shaken in 2021, when my father was diagnosed with colon cancer. This was incredibly hard for both of us, but he trusted me to support him through his fight with the disease, just as I had done during his stroke. When I was in the hospital with him, months before he passed, he told me that one of the reasons he came to faith was because he watched how I was living my life, following Jesus, loving my wife and children, and continuing to show up and serve people through Love Beyond Walls. I have an audio recording of him saying these things, and I still listen to it and will until I am no longer able.

On January 24, 2024, my father took his last breath. I somehow found the courage to preach his eulogy, since he asked me to when he was in the hospital.

Let me say this. I miss my dad. I miss the man I got to know. I am heartbroken that when we got close, I only had a small window of time with the person that everyone loved. I hate how his own trauma impacted him and caused him to make decisions that I needed to forgive him for. I wish we could have had more time together. I also hate what systemic injustice has done to many Black and Brown communities and how it has impacted so many people and left countless family connections in ruins, but I am also grateful for the powerful and glorious work of forgiveness and restoration.

My father became my number-one supporter and joined my community of support and faith, and I joined his. My father was there when I released my first traditionally published book, *I See You: How Love Opens Our Eyes to Invisible People*. He encouraged me when I decided to pursue my doctoral education later in life, and he celebrated with me when I defended my dissertation. This would be over twenty years after dropping out of high school and fighting to become who God had created me to be.

My dad at my book signing at Georgia Tech's Barnes and Noble store. I was a grown man with a family of my own, but having my father attend the bookstore signing for my first traditionally published book was deeply meaningful. Not only did I get to sign this book for him, but now the book is one of my most cherished possessions.

You know, one of the last things my father told me before he passed away was that I should always have a "forever forward" mentality. That, to me, is a perfect example of who he was. He was a creative, a leader, a trauma survivor, an innovator, and a business owner. He was also an entrepreneur with a magnetic personality. He took his limited resources, without a lot of community support, and always looked forward. I honor all parts of my father because I grew to realized that the moments that make us not as great as we should be are what make us human and worthy of God's love.

In fact, my father was one of the first people outside my wife and children to call me "Dr. Lester," and I will never forget this redemption; I promise to carry his "forever forward" message forward. Although he is not here to read this full story, I am at peace knowing that he would be honored to know that I am committed to carrying on his legacy. Much like the survivors of Tulsa, my family and I have navigated the lingering effects of systemic injustice.

I am convinced that God can break the chains of systemic injustice, generational trauma, and distance through faith, community, education, safe spaces to heal, and trauma-informed care. Why can't the collective power of community wrap its arms around a Tulsa survivor, a poverty survivor, a family trauma survivor, or any other person attempting to break through the pain of transgenerational trauma and educational injustice?

My personal journey has taught me invaluable lessons about perseverance, support, and the power of education in transforming lives. The ability to stay in school and complete my education was not just a personal victory; it was a testament to the importance of a strong, supportive community. Even when members of my community were from different walks of life, that somehow individually became the collective force to my life change and trajectory.

Rising from the ashes of poverty, trauma, and injustice during a time when Black and Brown people were experiencing the residue of Jim Crow in the 1980s and 1990s is also a testament to the collective *power* that can manifest when a community comes together. This collective power ensures that those suffering from lack, barriers, and unequal opportunities can find safety and courage to break the chains in community, even if that community is just one person or a whole group who believe in the power of God and are dedicated to helping those who need guidance and support at a critical time.

BECOMING COMMUNITY TO CREATE CHANGE

Through the work we've done at Love Beyond Walls, I have witnessed people transition from being unhoused to securing stable housing, from unemployment to gainful employment, from losing touch with family to reuniting with loved ones, and from dropping out of school to earning their GED or completing high school. How? Because a community stepped up.

If I truly believed that community was the answer, after my own life had been transformed by it, then I knew I had to *become* that community for those who needed it. Why? Because what good is it to obtain education and know what it takes to turn your life around, only to be self-serving? I believe that God allowed me to overcome in order to help others overcome as well. I wanted to become a community so as to create the change I wished to see. One of my favorite passages in the Bible says it this way:

> The Spirit of the Lord GOD is upon Me,
> Because the LORD has anointed Me
> To preach good tidings to the poor;
> He has sent Me to heal the brokenhearted,
> To proclaim liberty to the captives,
> And the opening of the prison to those who are bound;
> To proclaim the acceptable year of the LORD,
> And the day of vengeance of our God;
> To comfort all who mourn,
> To console those who mourn in Zion,
> To give them beauty for ashes,

The oil of joy for mourning,
The garment of praise for the spirit of heaviness;
That they may be called trees of righteousness,
The planting of the LORD, that He may be glorified.
       (Isaiah 61:1-3 NKJV)

This passage captures the essence of Jesus' mission, one that was not self-serving but focused on serving others and bringing restoration and liberation. When Jesus read these words in the synagogue (Luke 4:18-19), he declared that this Scripture was fulfilled in him, emphasizing that his purpose was to uplift the poor, heal the brokenhearted, and bring liberation and hope to those in despair. His life was the ultimate example of what it means to step into community, to meet people in their pain, and to help them find liberation and restoration. Following this example, I knew that my own transformation wasn't just for me—it was a call to be part of creating a community that mirrors the hope, restoration, and liberation that Jesus himself modeled.

In working in the spaces of poverty and homelessness and among vulnerable populations, I have learned that community needs to embody five basic elements if it is to be effective in helping people heal and overcome systemic and generational trauma, poverty, a lack of access to resources, or social deficits. These were the same elements, on a personal level, I shared with my own father and that he shared with me. Additionally, I am not unaware that some people will not be able to follow this for their own sense of safety and removing themselves from environments that have caused their trauma and causes them to be triggered. I was able to do this with support, years of therapy, inner work, and by working through emotional pain—seeking forgiveness for myself, practicing forgiveness toward others, and realizing that my story could empower me to show up in spaces that were

FIVE ELEMENTS OF COMMUNITY SUPPORT

Proximity—Proximity is more than support because proximity means that you are close enough to stand with people in their suffering. This does not mean carrying the suffering for people but helping to carry those who are suffering. Proximity is lamenting, standing in solidarity, committing to resist any form of injustice alongside others, and being willing to sacrifice to ensure the person facing injustice or pain is not alone. Scripture teaches us in Matthew 25:40, "Whatever you did for one of the least of these brothers and sisters of mine, you did for me."

Presence—Presence is different from proximity because presence is about awareness. It is about helping that person or community feel seen. Presence is about affirming a person or community's dignity and inherent worth. Our presence reassures others that they are not alone in their struggles. In educational settings, faith communities, personal relationships, and other support communities, a consistent presence can make a profound impact on people's lives.

Purpose—Purpose is about reminding people and communities that regardless of what they have endured, no amount of suffering can take away the fact that they have purpose. This aligns with Jeremiah 29:11, where God declares, "I know the plans I have for you, . . . plans to prosper you and not to harm you, plans to give you hope and a future." God is speaking through this major prophet to encourage God's people about his purpose for their lives, even though they were still in exile. By helping people to realize their worth and purpose, we empower them to see beyond their current circumstances.

Practice—Practice is about creating space for people to feel free to be themselves in order to overcome their struggles, without the pressures or judgment of trying to be perfect. Practice is about embodying what proximity, presence, and purpose is all about by walking alongside people in a way that reminds them that they are both worthy of support and worthy to be journeyed with, even when they make mistakes or fall short. It is true when Scripture says in James 2:17, "Faith by itself, if it is not accompanied by action, is dead." Through practice, we help people build resilience to overcome struggle, injustice, and heal through trauma.

Patience—The embodiment of patience is probably the most important element because it is about being long-suffering. The constancy of a community is what is needed to allow people to overcome and heal. And when I use the term heal, I am saying creating a safe space to process all that they have journeyed through. Communities need to give others the time to change and grow at their own pace while supporting them through their hardships. If you give up on a community or a person before change comes, how is this helpful? The Scriptures teach us in Galatians 6:9, "Let us not become weary in doing good, for at the proper time we will reap a harvest if we do not give up." Patience reminds us that transformation is a journey, not a quick fix.

tough and sometimes heavy. I urge you to seek professional support and wise counsel, engage in therapy, and position yourself in the best place to begin your healing journey—especially if you feel unprepared or find the process challenging. It is better to go with support than not have it all.

So, what will you do? Will you become the community that people need? Will you rethink how the church looks at people who are trying to be liberated? Will you commit to being a part of the change for those trying to escape trauma, injustice, and poverty after their lives have experienced ruin?

May we always be aware that people are waiting to find a community that will support them in a way that allows them to receive the help they need to experience the liberation necessary to live the life God has for them, whether it's becoming a PhD, healing, experiencing faith, or returning to their community to make a difference.

A MOMENT OF REFLECTION

This was the hardest chapter I have ever written. That is because I miss my father. It is also because I realize just how much the power of community changed my life. That community empowered me to do so many things: it helped me to succeed educationally, encouraged forgiveness, and helped me forge a friendship with my father before he took his last breath. I wish my father and I had more time to spend with each other. Is this your story? Or are you still navigating repair socially or in your own family? Are you still healing through trauma? Think about the role of community support in your own life. Who are those people you call community, and how have they helped you navigate life, faith, or through hardships? Have there been moments when the encouragement or presence of others have helped you overcome personal and systemic challenges? Did that empowerment drive you to make a difference in your community? How did these experiences shape your ability to extend grace and support to others, particularly those closest to you?

Reflect on the ways your personal journey has been influenced by both giving and receiving support through the power of community. Consider the impact of structural injustices on the lives of those around you or in your own life. Reflect on the resilience required to navigate these challenges and the importance of faith or trauma-informed support, especially within the context of strained familial relationships. Consider how the act of showing up can be used by God to bring forgiveness, healing, and transformation. Think about walking with someone who might need proximity, presence, purpose, practice, and patience. Who are those people? In what ways can you become their community?

We must become the change in this world for others to know it is possible to be liberated from suffering and systemic injustice. We must build a community where it is safe for people to heal, experience restoration, pursue education, and feel their worthiness and belonging. May you be moved to become a part of the transformative power of community and the critical role it plays in personal and collective healing. This is a call to action to become an active part of the community that God uses to ensure that everyone has the support they need to overcome their challenges and reach their full potential.

TEN

SAFE SPACES AND COMEBACK STORIES

O n May 9, 2024, I landed in Louisville, Kentucky, to attend a
press conference at Simmons College of Kentucky. Arriving
at the school, I saw that the conference had attracted some significant interest. Several news outlets were in attendance. So was
the mayor, a former congressman, the chief of police, and other
dignitaries standing alongside the college's leaders and faculty.

Simmons College of Kentucky was the last designated HBCU
to be established in the United States. Simmons was founded
after the Civil War in 1865 by twelve Black churches that were
members of the Kentucky State Convention of Colored Baptist
Churches. These churches had one purpose in mind: to ensure
that people who had been oppressed by white supremacy and injustice could have access to a post-secondary education or, in
other words, an education beyond high school.[1] This collection of
leaders and churches came together and purchased four acres of
land in Louisville to serve as the campus for the Kentucky Normal
and Theological Institute in 1879. William Simmons, an ex-slave,
became the second president of this historic college in 1880, after
the brief tenure of Elijah P. Marrs.[2] Under the leadership of
Simmons, the institute experienced growth and was later renamed Simmons University. By the 1900s, this university, originally built by former slaves, was offering degrees in both nursing
and law in conjunction with Louisville University.

However, the Great Depression, continual racial injustices, and a lack of resources ultimately would have a devastating impact on the school.[3] This impact resulted in the loss of the university's buildings and land, with only one program available to offer. In a turn of events, the University of Louisville decided to buy most of the property and created the Louisville Municipal College. This was to become U of L's Black branch of education under segregation.

Sadly, under the agreement of the sale, Simmons would only offer religious instruction. However, as unfortunate as that was, this branch of Black education would experience one of the greatest comebacks in educational history.[4] Indeed, it was this single program that enabled Simmons College to gain accreditation and be designated as the last HBCU in the country in 2015.[5] To qualify as a designated HBCU, an institution must have been established before 1965 and remained open continuously. Simmons College managed to stay open with just one program until its sitting president was able to lead it forward and put the college on a path to regain all of its former land and buildings. HBCUstory reported:

> Under the leadership of President Cosby, who took the helm seven years ago, Simmons has taken several steps to restore it to its original prominence. In 2007, the college regained its original campus after 77 years and relocated to its original site. In 2010, the institution attained candidate status with national accreditor ABHE, making it immediately eligible to receive federal funds under Title IV.
>
> It signed an articulation agreement with the University of Louisville and enjoys partnerships and agreements with Jefferson Community and Technical College, Spalding University and Campbellsville University. Simmons is a signature partner of the 55,000 Degrees, a community-wide

effort to add 40,000 bachelor's degrees and 15,000 associate's degrees in the Louisville Community by 2020.

Rev. C. B. Akins, a Simmons Trustee, said "The time was
right for Dr. Cosby to be at the helm of this school. If I told
him he could not swallow an elephant, he would say, 'I can
if I take one bite at a time.'"[6]

I cannot tell you how excited and overjoyed I felt to witness
this moment of such historical significance. But what exactly was
I doing there?

HOW I MADE IT TO SIMMONS COLLEGE
OF KENTUCKY

In fact, I was in Louisville that day to take my place alongside the
president of the college, the vice president, the mayor, a former
congressman, the chief of police, local leaders, and the faculty.
The press conference was the official announcement of my in-
volvement in creating a unique program that would serve the
most vulnerable people in Louisville, particularly those experiencing homelessness. This initiative aspired to provide pathways
into higher education for people facing homelessness and poverty.
I was there to be announced as the PhD and academic scholar who
would lead this effort at Simmons to help others make a comeback,
just as I had. I was also there to discuss collaboration opportunities with stakeholders, community organizations, and partners.

Yes: the PhD and academic scholar.

A conversation with my wife helped shape my decision to go back
to school again. I asked her if she thought I had what it took to
complete a doctorate. Without hesitation, she encouraged me and
said she could see me teaching one day because of my experiences
through the organization, speaking, and life events. With her and
my children's support, I applied to Union Institute and University,

founded in 1964, and focused on the adult learner with an emphasis on social connectedness, social justice, and social responsibility.[7] I applied to the social justice–focused PhD program with a concentration in public policy and social change, and I was accepted.

While working on my PhD at Union, I met Dr. Kevin Cosby, who was working on his second doctorate. I learned that Dr. Cosby had been the president of Simmons College of Kentucky for over twenty years and played a crucial role in its revitalization. I knew this because we took courses together and, in our class discussions, we would share our work with each other. And I would hear about the work of Simmons. At that time, it did not even cross my mind that, years after we had both graduated, Dr. Cosby would reach out to me and ask whether I wanted to join the faculty at Simmons, helping to direct and develop its public policy concentration under its interdisciplinary studies program and leading the Open Doors Initiative, which would provide college access to unhoused young adults.[8] We discussed this opportunity together at length, and because I had experienced a form of homelessness myself and had started the work of Love Beyond Walls, I accepted the roles of both director and professor while continuing to lead the nonprofit in Atlanta.

Now, standing there beside the university leaders in Louisville, I was overwhelmed with many emotions: sadness because my dad was not here to hear the news, and joy because I overcame my challenges. I reflected on my past trauma, my own times of struggling without a home, the moments I struggled as a high school dropout, and even the time I joined a gang in the hopes of finding belonging. Now I would be given the opportunity to lead this effort at Simmons to help others make a comeback, just like I had.

Just moments before I was to speak to the press, I couldn't help but think of that moment when I prayed, desperately wanting my purpose to not be overshadowed by generational trauma, systemic injustice, and how hard I had to fight to overcome both spiritual and physical poverty. I reflected on the people along the way who helped me find the resilience to overcome. My mother, Dr. Connie Walker, whose love was not always soft but who pushed me to overcome the systemic traps that were set up for me. I remembered the people who, while not my family, stepped in and filled critical roles during times I needed it the most; and I remembered the church, where I learned that nothing could separate me from the love of God. I couldn't have made this story up if I tried. But I know, ultimately, that it was all because of the grace of God.

My mind then began to shift toward the future. I realized that I had been put into a position to create a safe and healing environment for others. I wanted my words to cast a vision not just for the program itself but for those who were there listening or watching on television. The vision I wanted to cast was for all of us to really see those who have been historically marginalized and excluded—and to be a part of creating pathways and a safe space where people can become all that they dream. Where people can have their own comeback stories. Like I did, and like Simmons did.

This is why I named my talk at the press conference, "Creating Safe Educational Spaces for People to Make a Comeback," especially in light of the Supreme Court ruling surrounding *Grants Pass v. Johnson*, where justices said that it was constitutional for cities and states to create laws to make homelessness a crime nationally, even when people do not have access to a bed, shelter, or the resources needed to survive homelessness.[9] Here are a few lines I spoke that day:

> My questions today are: How do you have a comeback when the resources are few and public sanitation issues are widespread? How do you have a comeback when you are a target, and your experiences with homelessness have been used to create more invisibility?

I'll tell you, you can't—because doors are closed. Doors are closed when you try to enter a space to wash your hands. Doors are closed when you try to access public spaces or find limited beds. And doors are closed when you attempt to gain access, but hygiene gets in the way because you don't have an address. Doors close when you try to apply for a job, enroll in school, or attend college but cannot give an address.

We are dreaming about creating a program at Simmons that would open its doors to help young adults and non-traditional prospective students experiencing homelessness have access to college. The first of its kind at an HBCU, which is both historic and important because fifty percent of that population is Black and Brown. Education is also a pathway to empowerment. Think if each college across this country would open its doors to ensure that people could seek education as a pathway out of homelessness.

CREATING SPACE

If we adopt this type of lens, we would be more intentional in supporting K–12 students and community members struggling with poverty and systemic or educational injustice. Safe spaces are not just physical places. They can also be emotional sanctuaries, where people can express themselves without fear of judgment or exclusion. Over the years, I've come to understand that trauma is something we all experience and that affects us all in some way or another. I have experienced trauma, and I am sure you have too. It is impactful and can take many forms. Transgenerational trauma, in particular, hinders people from reaching their full potential, including their educational potential. Creating these types of safe spaces is a form of reparations, an investment in educational access and the creation of environments where people can find community and heal together. When I say "safe space," I refer to how it is defined in the SAFE Spaces: Framework for Healing Environments table.

Each type of space in the table offers unique opportunities for healing, prioritizing holistic wellness that counters the deprivations of poverty.

SAFE SPACES Framework for healing environments		
Acronym	Explanation	Details
S Socially aware	■ Acknowledging the impact of systemic injustice on people's lives and stories. ■ Being a community of education rather than a community that ignores historical and current injustices. ■ Supporting or starting initiatives that address these issues directly.	Establishing spaces that do not ignore or dismiss historical and present injustices. These environments actively recognize and address the connections between past and present traumas caused by systemic or educational injustices.
A Affirming	■ Affirming the worth, stories, and humanity of people's experiences. ■ Having inclusive practices that respect diversity in all forms, ensuring that people can be whole. ■ Creating safety where vulnerable conversations can happen organically.	Creating a supportive and validating atmosphere for people's experiences. Cultivating trust and a sense of belonging is crucial for healing.
F Fair/just	■ Fighting for equitable access to resources, opportunities, and support—with fairness and justice. ■ Making equity and justice core values. ■ Actively working to remove barriers that contribute to inequality.	Ensuring that everyone has equitable access to resources, opportunities, and support. Fairness is about justice and equity, and involves actively working to dismantle barriers created by systemic injustices and upholding equal treatment for all.
E Environments focused on healing	■ Providing access to mental health support or programming and trauma-informed care. ■ Creating safe physical spaces for reflection, healing, support, and recovery. ■ Building a community that supports continuous healing and growth in resistance to injustice.	Developing physical and emotional spaces designed for healing and well-being. This includes providing access to mental health resources or building communal connections for resources to be shared with those who are unable to afford them. Additionally, this is where people can find a community in order to process and recover from trauma.

CHURCHES AND FAITH COMMUNITIES

Churches and faith communities have an opportunity to do significant work by creating community-led support groups that could serve as a form of guidance and a healthy approach to teaching for those who identify as Christian. Or they could offer spiritually grounding programs and practices that help to develop a person's spiritual health, led by both strong leaders and compassionate congregants or attendees. Because I am a part of the Christian tradition, I believe groups in a sacred space could facilitate conversations and provide space for those experiencing systemic trauma while also experiencing the love of God.

It is clear that the concept of creating safe spaces can be found in the text of Scripture, as Paul writes, "Bear one another's burdens, and so fulfill the law of Christ" (Galatians 6:2 ESV). Imagine if more churches became places of belonging, where people felt safe enough to heal, instead of being perceived as places of judgement and criticism. Paul also writes, "Encourage one another and build one another up, just as you are doing" (1 Thessalonians 5:11 ESV).

I believe that evangelical churches and faith communities have missed the opportunity to lead in addressing injustice due to prevalent judgment and hatred within the forms of church that elevate White Christian nationalism over liberation, and judgment over justice. This is compounded by ignorance about historical injustices and systemic issues, which prevents the creation of spaces where people can lament and fully process the impacts of injustice. However, if churches embraced their role as sanctuaries of healing and acceptance, they could transform lives and whole communities.

It seems to be a theme in Scripture that community is where healing can take place. Consider this passage: "Let us consider how to stir up one another to love and good works, not neglecting to meet together, as is the habit of some, but encouraging one another, and all the more as you see the Day drawing near"

(Hebrews 10:24-25 ESV). By embracing this wisdom and implementing evidence-based practices, many churches and faith communities would be equipped to create environments where healing and growth are possible.

SCHOOLS

Schools have an incredible opportunity to create spaces where students can heal and be seen. When I was an educator in the school system, I co-started two groups for students: one called the Trailblazers for young men, the other called the Pathfinders for young women. The social worker, school counselors, a parent liaison, and I were all involved in these groups designed for students from impoverished backgrounds who had trouble connecting with their lessons and who had found themselves, as I once did, getting into trouble. Every week after school, the parent liaison, Ms. Jackson, would lead the group of young ladies with the female school counselor, while I facilitated the male group with the male school social worker and the school counselor. Additionally, I built relationships with parent volunteers and asked whether they would come to speak to the entire group during school hours.

Each time we met, the principal would allow us an hour to meet with the students before school started, after, and sometimes during classes to inspire these students. I regularly invited parents and community leaders, business owners, creatives, and others with whom they wouldn't normally have contact to speak with them in their groups. Because of its initial success, this group grew from 10 students in both groups to over 150 students. This is important because it showed that the students longed for a community where they could feel like they were a part of something and not isolated. Additionally, doing this work, the teachers, counselors, social worker, and administration saw tremendous improvements in these students, behaviorally and sometimes academically. We also found that the students learned ways to cope and manage their experiences from the pressures stemming from their neighborhoods and community, and the group became a pathway for them to receive extra support and resources, like tutoring and extra-credit assignments. It was their comeback moment. The success of these groups reveals the transformative power of community and support in educational settings in the face of educational injustice. This was a form of social change work and ministry that I will never forget.

Can you imagine if every school system around the country and the world trained their educators to be trauma informed and teach from a trauma-informed care and pedagogy lens? The potential impact on student success and well-being would be immeasurable. Educators trained in trauma-informed practices have the ability to create environments where all students feel safe, supported, and empowered to succeed.

COMMUNITY

Could you imagine how access to wellness from a holistic standpoint could help heal the mental and social health of those who have had to journey through injustice? Community wellness initiatives could include mental health services, physical health programs, and social support networks, which would address the diverse needs of community members. It is wellness and community itself that have given me the greatest chance of having a comeback story. Why? Because wellness is what can help our communities heal and resist all that systemic injustices have done. By investing in community wellness, we are investing in the future of our society. It has been wellness, resilience, faith, and community that saved my life. Being healthy (not perfect) in each of these areas gave me a healthier relationship with my mother, Dr. Connie; saw my dad, Tyrone, change his life; and had me at an HBCU being named something that I would have never imagined of being named: a director and professor. I believe that it is time for all of us to see wellness and trauma care as necessary not only to help in overall healing but also to improve relationships and communities.

Although the program is still in its beginning stages, the Open Doors Initiative will be the first of its kind at an HBCU in the United States committed to this type of work. I have worked hard and have developed the school's Public Policy and Social Change concentration, part of the Interdisciplinary Studies degree program. It contains six courses, ranging from Policy and Social Power, Understanding Homelessness and Social Stigma, to Humanizing Marginalized Communities, that will support students as they think about how they can become change agents in the fields of policy, homelessness, mass incarceration, educational disparities and injustices, climate change and environmental racism, and any field that interests them. It is my hope that this helps to raise up student leaders who will embody what it means to open doors. This initiative is similar to the University of Southern California (USC) Street Medicine program, which provides health care services to the homeless population, including access to medical care, mental health support, and social services.[10] However, while USC's program focuses on health, Simmons College's Open Doors Initiative integrates educational access with comprehensive support services for unhoused young adults to use education as a means to provide housing, community, counseling, and the necessary communal support and training to become self-sufficient leaders.

I believe that transformation could be a reality for millions of people—if we commit to creating and sustaining these supportive environments that create space for those who feel overlooked and excluded because of any type of injustice—especially educational injustice.

- Will you join this type of work? How?
- Will you become an advocate for justice in a way that ensures others can access higher education?
- Will you lead your community of faith in a way that shows the love of God by creating safe spaces for those trying to overcome systemic challenges and heal?
- Will you commit to investing in the next generation of students who do not have the resources, community support, or economic means to become the first in their families to graduate from college? What could that look like?

It is more than just knowing the context I have outlined by covering history and being vulnerable by sharing my story. We must not expect those who are struggling to find a community by themselves. We must become that community for them. We will be their community through the way that we live and by involving ourselves in the lives of those who suffer. We must understand that this is a long journey. It took me twenty years to go from where I was to who I am today. And I am committed to pouring myself back into those who will follow. But I can't do it alone.

Education is one of the many ways people can use to overcome. I believe we need to designate more Black scholars who can tell their stories of overcoming—scholars who came from environments littered with pain and trauma—to give hope to those who are struggling. They must believe it is possible for them too.

WHAT IT TAKES TO HAVE A COMEBACK

When Cecilia and I cofounded Love Beyond Walls, one of the first people I met was a man named James. I met James after living on the streets for a while as a public demonstration to stand in solidarity for those who were unhoused in Atlanta. James, at the time, was living under a bridge. Underneath this bridge, in the heart of the city, were a lot of people living in tents. It had once been known as Atlanta's Tent City. People from all walks of life and life experiences lived under this bridge. It was filled with tons of jagged rocks, making it an unbearable place to sleep, unless you had a large number of blankets and a lot of cardboard.

One of my first campaigns with Love Beyond Walls involved living on the streets of Atlanta in December 2013 to experience firsthand what people who are unhoused go through each day. Before attempting to live a few days on the street, I spoke with my family to get their blessing. With their permission, they dropped me off underneath a bridge three days before Christmas and allowed me to live on the streets in an encampment. James was one of the first people who greeted me, shared his blankets and food, and introduced me to the whole community. Because I was upfront about the fact that I was there not because I was unhoused but because, by spending time with them and in the conditions they endured, I would raise awareness of their struggle, I was welcomed into this community.

After this awareness campaign and demonstration, Love Beyond Walls came alongside James in support until he was able to get off the streets, reunite with his daughter, and eventually get a job and his own apartment. After James got more stable, I had a chance to learn more about his story.

He also introduced me to his younger brother, Mike. Both brothers shared with me that they had been exposed to drugs at a very young age on account of their mother being addicted to heroin and what was called crack cocaine. Mike, who was twenty-one at the time, had never finished school and had been experiencing acute homelessness. Because of his early drug exposure, he had living from place to place from the age of sixteen. James and Mike's story was heartbreaking. James told me how he and Mike had to take care of one another from an early age. Even though, at times, James struggled with his own addiction, he continued to check in on his brother, even though they were having different experiences with homelessness.

During their younger years, they were often left without food and proper care. This pushed them onto the streets, where they encountered dangerous and negative influences. Both of them eventually dropped out of school. Despite these challenges, James remained protective of his younger brother and always tried to shield him from the worst of their circumstances. It was clear that James cared deeply for Mike's future, even at the expense of his own, and he would always tell him when we were all present that he wanted him to finish school someday.

One day, I found the courage to ask Mike about his dream of going back to school. He agreed it was his dream to obtain his GED, since he had missed the opportunity to complete high school in the traditional sense. I was excited to hear that he wanted to obtain a nontraditional form of education that he could leverage for his own personal growth and development. Mike's dream made me think of a friend of mine named Alex, who helped young Black men and women finish their high school education. Alex would help young people like Mike find resources to pay for their GED study materials. He also supported them through their education journeys by helping them find sustainable housing, pairing them with study partners and tutors, and providing paid internships while they completed high school.

Helping Mike achieve his dream of going back to school did not happen quickly. It was a process to track down his transcripts from high school, get identification for him, and make sure he was stable before he could start. The process of getting his identification held everything up because he needed to verify who he was and didn't have a clear way to do so, until we stepped in and assisted him with hiring an attorney to help him with that process. Almost a year after meeting Mike and introducing him to Alex, Alex was able to mobilize a community to surround Mike with tutors, housing, mental health counseling, monetary support, and a space to heal.

Mike eventually received his GED with the support of a powerful community of people who were willing to journey with him. Mike now has a job and stable housing, just because I paused long enough to hear a story that wasn't my own. Mike's story had me connect with Alex, and then Alex was willing to become the community Mike needed, and it changed the trajectory of his life forever.

Overcoming struggle and oppression requires more than what a person in deficit might have. It takes people standing with you in ways you cannot stand for yourself. It takes listening to stories. It takes suffering with people and embracing solidarity as a superpower. It means realizing that the power of a supportive community cannot be overstated because it is at the heart of what it takes to break the chains of injustice. A community that stands together in solidarity has the ability to lift people out of the depths of despair, homelessness, poverty, oppression, doubt, and trauma, and guide them toward a future that is filled with healing and purpose. In essence, community can become the soil in which we are planted and—if in the right environment—it can be capable of nurturing and feeding us. It is then that we can grow and thrive, becoming all that God wants us to be.

The more we are robbed of the richness of that soil, the richness of community, the richness of care and concern, the greater the chances of withering. Just as a rose needs rich soil in order to burst through the oppressive concrete and bloom, a community can become that soil, offering love, support, and understanding. Whether it's through providing education, emotional support, or simply being present, the power of community is a testament to the resilience of the human spirit and what the psalmist David said: "God sets the solitary in families" (Psalm 68:6 NKJV). When people are truly and authentically embraced by a caring community, they are empowered to heal and, ultimately, grow. In moments of darkness and trauma, it is often the community that brings light, reminding people they are not alone. They are seen, and they know they have worth and are loved. Being a part of a caring community can make systemic and social change possible. Knowing this is how we can start a chain reaction by showing how to cultivate spaces to help break the chains of injustice and educational injustice.

This is the power of community.

THIS IS HAPPENING

I gave myself a pep talk. "Terence, you got this. This is happening." We walked, slowly and single file, toward the stage. In the crowd I saw my mother, Dr. Connie Walker, my wife, Cecilia, my children, Zion and TJ, my older sister, Dr. Monica Lester, all of whom had flown in to witness me—my dad was alive but sick and could not make it. However, I was on the phone with him the entire time. They were snapping pictures. My hands were sweaty, and the heat from the heavy regalia didn't help.

It was July 9, 2023. I had flown to Cincinnati, Ohio, the night before and had laid out my clothes before going to sleep. I had arrived at the convention space, fighting through my disbelief.

Looking back, I was grateful to my dissertation committee for believing in me and supporting me through this journey, especially Dr. Ralph Watkins, who was the pastor of Wheat Street Baptist Church—the same church my grandmother took me to as a child and the same church where I later worked alongside him for a season as a pastor of social justice and witness. Dr. Jennifer Raymond, the academic dean of the PhD program, believed in my work and became a source of encouragement, drawing from her years of experience in policy, homelessness, and housing advocacy. Dr. Baird, my professor of policy and my dissertation chair, was a tremendous support throughout my research, meeting with me each week to guide and challenge my thinking.

The committee members' belief in my work and unwavering support carried me through some of the most difficult moments of this journey. Each, in their own way, reinforced the importance of scholarship that is deeply connected to justice, advocacy, and lived experience. Their guidance not only shaped my research but also deepened my commitment to using academia as a tool for systemic change.

Now, I was standing in a long line of graduates preparing to walk across the stage. I was ready to receive my PhD.

When I finally made it to my seat among the PhD candidates, I glanced back and saw my family again. The weight of the moment dawned on me. This was a dream, and it was coming true. In that moment, I cried uncontrollable tears looking at their smiling faces.

How in the world had I gotten here? A Black kid from Campbellton Road, raised in poverty in the city of Atlanta, who had joined a street gang as a teenager and experienced brief homelessness and hopelessness, was now about to receive one of the highest educational degrees—the first man in my family to do so. For someone like me, with a life that fell so far outside the traditional path to higher education or a terminal degree like a PhD, a reality like this doesn't just happen.

But then it happened. I walked on that stage, one of the few Black people to walk that day, and got hooded by my dissertation chair, Dr. Karen Baird.

This was a point of demarcation for me. And perhaps most meaningful of all, this moment was powerful for my children, Zion and TJ, to witness—my ceiling becoming their floor. The demeaning words of my awful warehouse supervisor even flashed through my mind. But I had proved him wrong. I had overcome the social stigma that he held in his mind toward young Black men. The weight of years of impostor syndrome seemed to lift away; the burden of trauma and abuse felt lighter. I was not the statistic that society or some of my former educators expected me to become. My life was almost upended by the many hardships that came of growing up in social conditions that were littered with lack and poverty. But I had broken through.

My story is an anomaly, but it does not have to be. Many don't have a moment like this because, as this book has illustrated, growing up in an urban context can be immensely heavy and isolating, littered with few resources, little guidance, and educational injustice. It is hard, and it can feel even harder to escape. Yet after a childhood marked by poverty, depression, abuse, and trauma, I had ended up here, receiving a doctorate. I had defended a dissertation that has added to the literature of the academy on harmful policies that criminalize and publicly sanitize the poor and unhoused.[1] *I was also a community leader, married for almost two decades, with two beautiful children.*

I will never forget my mother's words when I joined my family afterward: "I am proud of the man you have become . . ." My wife and children watched my mother and me embrace; recalling this moment still brings me to

My wife, children, mother, sister, my wife's sister and niece, and my dissertation chair with me after graduation.

tears. After all, watching my mother endure and also obtain a doctorate was one of my greatest examples and motivators.

MY HOPE

I hope my words have helped you to understand why PhDs don't come from places where I am from and what we need to do to ensure that they do. People are suffering and trying their best to escape the barriers that have hindered their attempts to escape poverty and claimed the lives of those who were, and are, just trying to survive. I am compelled to share my belief that it is with community that people can overcome their challenges and resist the systemic and social barriers that hold them back. My words have been a call to see more roses break through the concrete and into a future where equity in education and other personal goals or dreams are not the exception but the norm—where every child has the chance to reach their potential.

I found inspiration in education with the support of a healthy community. I realized that education was a way for me to find myself and to reclaim my mind, voice, and history. I also developed the belief that we can and must help those who find themselves unable to break through the barriers of systemic injustice.

I still sometimes take long rides through the Ben Hill community. I still see decay in areas untouched by redevelopment. The dilapidated buildings on certain parts of the road are silent witnesses to both the resilience and despair of those living there, with some of the same people standing on the corners and news of others who have died prematurely. These reflections both contain my personal journey and bring attention to the ongoing struggles in these communities. I even went back there to take my graduation pictures to symbolize the growth that had occurred and made a social post that said I did it for "the hood," literally.

It is my hope that we will one day have more Black and Brown representation in PhD programs as scholars, and that we see more Black brilliance gracing the academic hallways and environments, as set forth by people like Edward Bouchet, the first Black person to complete a PhD in the late 1800s.[2] One day, I hope, we will use our brilliance to add to the scholarship in the academy, instead of being a small percentage in the academy or only valued as data for researchers who come to our communities for the sake of research interests, while people wither away under the concrete. Black and Brown scholarship matters. Our collective journey toward this dream of hope

With my PhD hood in the old neighborhood.

and change begins with acknowledging these truths, understanding the depth of their impact, and committing to act with empathy and resolve.

A HEARTFELT POEM

This piece of original poetry speaks to my journey and how community saved my life. It is my hope that this poem speaks to you and will cause you to reflect on the many roses who need that opportunity to push through their own personal concrete and grow through the pain and trauma before them to become who God made them to be. Think about the communities you are a part of. Consider the ways in which you can contribute to creating environments where others can heal and grow.

The Rose That Came Back

Can you see the rose that has been stepped on and crushed,
Left in the dust to rot and dry?
No water around to feel or handle its cry.
Can you see the way the storm has come and showered
    its rain,
Thunder and lightning so loud you cannot hear its pain?
But then and only then, a ray pierces through the clouds,
A sound of hope when birds sing aloud.
Could it be that after the rain, the sun can work its wonders
And wipe the tears from the rain?
Could it be that the sun's rays,
so delicate and grace-filled,
Could help this rose rise from the trauma and heal?
Then there is also the soil it's in, contaminated by
    the environment
That was toxified by injustice.
But don't you worry, says the cloud and the rain,
Slowly it falls again
Helping to wash the pain away.
The elements become a sacred community
That allows this rose to experience liberation and immunity.
When we think that the steps of history have damaged
    its future,
We look again and see all of heaven conspiring for its
    growth from the rain.
Then comes the night and adds some more elements,
The breeze, the stars, the moon all scream,
This place where you are will not be your end.

Because as it is written in the book, Joy will come in the
    morning again.
Day after day, the rose continued to face hope
That a brighter tomorrow would replace the pain.
And it never gave up hope because the weather and
    the elements
Caused it to grow.
And that is what it did—it grew and grew
Through the rain, the toxic environment, and the dew.
That rose never looked back after all it had gone through,
And was suddenly picked after it grew from the rays and
    the hues.
Now handed to a generation to tell its story to other
    stepped-on roses,
May they hear the testimony from Glory that God can and
    will provide a comeback story.
The petals, once bruised, now shine with renewed strength,
A testament to resilience and the journey's length.
Roots dug deep in the soil of adversity,
Drawing strength from the depths of shared dignity
    and humanity.
The morning dew whispers horror stories of survival,
Each drop a reminder of the rose's revival.
In the still night, where hope silently creeps,
The rose finds peace and knows that God's promise is one
    God keeps.
Its leaves, once withered, now reach for the sky,
A symbol of faith that refuses to die.
So, to all who feel crushed by the weight of despair,
Look to the rose, its journey laid out for all to see and care.
For in every heart lies a seed of potential,
With love and support, its growth is essential.

And when the time comes for the rose to inspire,
May its story spark a courageous inner fire.
In those who are struggling, feeling outcast,
Know that with faith and hope, this too shall pass.
For the rose that came back from the concrete that oppressed
almost to the point of decay,
Teaches us all to believe fight for equity, stand in solidarity,
and to pray.
That no matter the trauma, trials, no matter the strife,
We can all bloom and reach our educational heights.
This is what we call, *A Rose That Came Back!*

ACKNOWLEDGMENTS

Frederick Douglass, the former slave who taught himself to read and later turned abolitionist, social reformer, writer, and lecturer, once spoke these words:

> If there is no struggle, there is no progress. Those who profess to favor freedom, and yet depreciate agitation, are men who want crops without plowing up the ground. They want rain without thunder and lightning. They want the ocean without the awful roar of its many waters.
>
> This struggle may be a moral one, or it may be a physical one, and it may be both moral and physical, but it must be a struggle. Power concedes nothing without a demand. It never did and it never will.[1]

These words both inspire and haunt me because, in reality, no one wants the pain that is associated with struggle. Yet somehow it is the struggle itself that has within it the liberation needed to overcome any obstacles. Writing this book has been a struggle, but as I have poured my heart out on these pages, I am also reminded of the great triumphs, revelations, and healing moments I have had. And that, as Douglass says, grants a type of internal progress that I believe is nameless and priceless. Struggle is hard, but when progress is made, you are able to appreciate that the struggle itself did not take you out but caused you to truly understand the power, resilience, and faith you had inside of you all along.

With this in mind, I want to thank and appreciate those people who have both stood with me during times of struggle and those who have been a part of my life in some meaningful way as I have journeyed from the depths of emotional and physical poverty, trauma, and hardship to become who I am today. It is the miracle of God that progress can be pulled out of struggle in this way. It has not been an easy journey, but I am thankful that somehow my struggle has produced in me the change needed to create a legacy that will be carried out through our children one day.

In adoration, I acknowledge my family and the people who have become like family to me. Thanks to my wife, Cecilia Lester, my daughter, Zion Joy Lester, and my son, Terence "TJ" Lester II. When I was journeying with my father in the hospital and finding the courage to write this book in the midst of my grief, it was you all that became my light and joy and helped me continue moving forward. I thank you for always being there for and with me. Cecilia, you are my best friend, and I wouldn't want to journey through this life of struggle with anyone else. Zion, I am glad to call you my coauthor and was honored to write our first children's book, *Zion Learns to See*, together. TJ, I am grateful to call you my brilliant son and my favorite basketball player. I believe that you will become a great thinker and leader. You all are my heart, and there is nothing that I have accomplished that hasn't had your support surrounding it all.

I thank my mother, Dr. Connie Walker, for pushing me when I was trying to find my way at a young age. You model to me resilience, fortitude, and strength, even as you overcame your own struggles. Many thanks, too, to my stepfather, Dewitt Walker Sr., for always believing that I had what it took to reach my potential. I consider you a father figure and will always see you as a positive role model and example to follow. You have been with me in some of my most crucial moments in life, when I was just trying to figure out my path.

I thank my sister, Dr. Monica Lester. You have been a support system, friend, and inspiration to me as I journeyed through graduate school, the loss of our father, and trying to figure out how to navigate all that life has thrown our way. You mean a lot to me, and I am grateful for you and the bond we have established.

Thank you to my sister Ashley, who was right by my side in the hospital, helping to care for our father, and who remained steadfast through the hardest days, leading us through the grief we endured—I thank God for you. I cherish our moments at the graveside of our father and the times at events where we retell his jokes to feel his presence again. Your love and strength have been a source of comfort, and I am forever grateful for you.

Carmelo O'Neal, I know Ty would be so proud of the athlete and young man you are becoming. I wish you success as you continue to grow in football and in your future career—keep striving for greatness! Remember, Ty is always with you in spirit.

Thanks to my grandparents, Carlton and Gloria York, and the late Herman Lester Sr. and Jessica Lester, for sowing the seeds of longevity, grit, and wisdom in my life. I want to thank my friend Broderick McBride. Brother, I thank you for calling me every single day to pray with me and for me as I journeyed through my grief after my father made his transition. I also thank you for allowing me to show up as my whole self to work through whatever I needed to as I grieved. I thank God for you.

I would like to thank my assistant Melanie Wittenberg. Thank you for your support in this work, for the way you encourage my family, and for your kind heart. May God continue to bless you.

I thank Mashaun Simon and Billy Honor for being friends and brothers. You both have inspired me and believed in me, and our brotherhood means a lot to me.

Thank you to Pastor Broderick Santiago, who stood by my side as I found the courage to be my father's caregiver and as a fellow minister at my father's funeral, when I gave my father's eulogy after his long battle. I will always remember the ways in which your support has inspired my wife and me over the years. I thank my friend and colleague Matthew Gibson, who on days when I needed inspiration showed up to help me create and keep leading the work God started in us at Love Beyond Walls and filmed my father's funeral.

To my brother Ron Wright, we spoke almost every day after my dad passed. As the Bible says, you became a brother born for adversity, but I would add you were also a brother for grief. I will never forget you sharing your experience after losing your mother and walking me through the grief process while I was in the trenches of my own.

I'd also like to thank my book agent, Trinity McFadden, who reached out and helped me to find a space for these words. It has been a long road, but I hope that one day my words will reach people all around the world. Thank you for your belief in me. Thanks to my former book agent, Tawny Johnson, who retired but still committed to look over my words and who encouraged me as I wrote with vulnerability.

Special thanks to my editor, Al Hsu, for believing in yet another book. I cannot believe that this is book five with the same publisher and book four with you. I am grateful that you have always been a believer in my work and words. Thank you for journeying with me in my writing career.

A special thank you to the whole InterVarsity Press family. You all have believed in me and my work since day one, and I thank you for giving me space to write about my stories, my life, and ways in which I see the world through the lens of dignity and compassion.

I'd like to thank one of my closest friends, Harvey Strickland, and his wife, Takeisha Strickland, and their children. Harvey, I am forever grateful for the initial work and support that you gave Cecilia and me to start the work at Love Beyond Walls. It is my hope that God has more for us all to do—together.

Thanks to the Love Beyond Walls team, to every donor, supporter, advocate, volunteer, and partner who has ever served and all those who have stood with our advocacy work over the years. Thank you all for being a part of a movement of doers.

Thank you to my friend Dr. Jemar Tisby, who is not only a colleague in the present moment at Simmons but also a friend, brother, and the writer of the foreword to this book, for seeing my story as something that is needed in this world.

Thank you all for supporting and following my writing journey. I am forever grateful.

NOTES

INTRODUCTION: WHEN ROSES GROW FROM CONCRETE

[1]Tupac Shakur, *The Rose That Grew from Concrete* (Poetry Collection) (New York: MTV Books, 2009).

[2]Meeyoung O. Min et al., "Factor Structure of the Urban Hassles Index," *Research on Social Work Practice* 28, no. 6 (2018): 741-50; David B. Miller and Aloen Townsend, "Urban Hassles as Chronic Stressors and Adolescent Mental Health: The Urban Hassles Index," *Brief Treatment and Crisis Intervention* 5, no. 1 (2005): 85-94.

[3]Shakur, *The Rose That Grew from Concrete*, 113.

[4]Joy DeGruy, *Post Traumatic Slave Syndrome: America's Legacy of Enduring Injury and Healing* (Milwaukie, OR: Uptone Press, 2005).

[5]Gregory Jantz, "Overcoming Childhood Traumatic Grief," The Center: A Place of HOPE, December 16, 2024, www.aplaceofhope.com/overcoming-childhood -traumatic-grief.

[6]*Trauma inheritance*, sometimes called *intergenerational* or *transgenerational trauma*, is when the impact of trauma gets passed down from one generation to the next.

1. THE INCIDENT

[1]Steve Rose, "Ruby Bridges: The Six-Year-Old Who Defied a Mob and Desegregated Her School," *The Guardian*, May 6, 2021, www.theguardian.com /society/2021/may/06/ruby-bridges-the-six-year-old-who-defied-a-mob-and -desegregated-her-school.

[2]National Museum of African American History and Culture, "Race and Racial Identity," accessed June 26, 2024, https://nmaahc.si.edu/learn/talking-about -race/topics/race-and-racial-identity.

[3]A "Grady Baby" is someone born at Grady Memorial Hospital in Atlanta—a term rooted in African American vernacular and carrying a powerful sense of

identity in the city. It's not just about where you were born; being a Grady Baby connects you to the soul of Atlanta, to generations who've come through Grady's doors, often as the only option in a once-segregated city. For many Black Atlantans, it symbolizes resilience, community, and pride, marking a legacy that is intertwined with the struggles and triumphs of the city's history.

[4]Conor Lee, "The Grady Hospital," *History Atlanta*, November 3, 2015, https://historyatlanta.com/the-grady-hospital/.

[5]Brendan P. Lovasik et al., "'The Living Monument': The Desegregation of Grady Memorial Hospital and the Changing South," *The American Surgeon* 86, no. 3 (2020): 213-19, https://doi.org/10.1177/000313482008600330.

[6]Lovasik et al., "'The Living Monument,'" abstract.

[7]"The History of Crack Cocaine in the US," Atlanta Detox Treatment Center, last modified June 19, 2023, https://atlantadetoxtreatment.com/2023/06/19/the-history-of-crack-cocaine/.

[8]Frederick Allen, *Atlanta Rising: The Invention of an International City 1946–1996* (Atlanta: Longstreet Press, 1996).

[9]Ronald H. Baylor, *Race and the Shaping of Twentieth-Century Atlanta* (Chapel Hill: The University of North Carolina Press, 2000), 130.

[10]Rachel Singh, "Atlanta Streets: When Roads Become Walls," Atlanta History Center, March 11, 2022, www.atlantahistorycenter.com/blog/atlanta-street-names-when-roads-become-walls.

[11]Fast-forward to today, when many parts of Campbellton Road feature affluent Black families, significant Black progress, successful schools, and numerous Black professionals, including entrepreneurs, professors, educators, doctors, and lawyers. However, there are still areas where Black poverty persists. I do not want to suggest that Black people never overcame and progressed, but I intend to reflect on what I remember from my childhood.

[12]"Census Bureau Reports 1980 Poverty Statistics," *New York Times*, August 22, 1982, www.nytimes.com/1982/08/22/us/census-bureau-reports-1980-poverty-statistics.html.

[13]David Pendered, "Fort McPherson Area Rich in Human Rights History, Poor in Redevelopment," SaportaReport, July 14, 2014, https://saportareport.com/fort-mcpherson-area-rich-in-human-rights-history-poor-in-redevelopment/columnists/david/david.

[14]Pendered, "Fort McPherson Area."

[15]Atlanta remains heavily populated with Black people, where the disparity is ever present and ever growing. Poverty rates among Black people are high.

Simultaneously, the city is known for Black affluence, and neighborhoods have been and continue to be gentrified.

[16]Rich Schapiro, Jon Schuppe, Simone Weichselbaum, and Safia Samee Ali, "Memphis Police Chief Once Led the Aggressive 'Red Dog' Anti-Crime Unit in Atlanta," *NBC News*, February 2, 2023, www.nbcnews.com/news/us-news/memphis-police-chief-cerelyn-cj-davis-atlanta-red-dog-rcna67674.

[17]A food desert is an area, often in impoverished communities, where access to affordable, nutritious food is scarce or nonexistent, forcing residents to rely on unhealthy, processed options.

[18]Grandmaster Flash and the Furious Five, "The Message," Sugarhill Records, YouTube video, August 24, 2015, 5:59, www.youtube.com/watch?v=Pobr SpMwKk4.

[19]Ta-Nehisi Coates, *Between the World and Me* (New York: Random House, 2015), 17.

[20]"The trap" is African American vernacular for a part of the neighborhood that is known for high crime rates, drugs, poverty, and a host of things that make escaping it almost impossible.

[21]James W. Loewen, *Lies My Teacher Told Me: Everything Your American History Textbook Got Wrong* (New York: Simon & Schuster, 1996). Loewen in this text does a great job at highlighting this phenomenon.

[22]Joy DeGruy, *Post Traumatic Slave Syndrome: America's Legacy of Enduring Injury and Healing* (Milwaukie, OR: Uptone Press, 2005), 13-14.

[23]DeGruy, *Post Traumatic Slave Syndrome*, 14.

[24]Ruth K. Thompson-Miller, "Jim Crow's Legacy: Segregation Stress Syndrome" (PhD diss., Texas A&M University, 2011), iii-iv.

[25]In fact, a Jim Crow Museum was created to educate people about the specific impact and the laws that affected millions of people and has examples of these laws by state. "Examples of Jim Crow Laws—Oct. 1960," Jim Crow Museum, accessed June 21, 2024, https://jimcrowmuseum.ferris.edu/links/misclink/examples.htm.

[26]Malik Simba, "The Three-Fifths Clause of the United States Constitution (1787)," Black Past, October 3, 2014, www.blackpast.org/african-american-history/events-african-american-history/three-fifths-clause-united-states-constitution-1787/.

[27]The White House, "Ending Radical and Wasteful Government DEI Programs and Preferencing," Presidential Actions, executive order, January 20, 2025, www.whitehouse.gov/presidential-actions/2025/01/ending-radical-and-wasteful-government-dei-programs-and-preferencing/.

[28]Tara Copp, "More DEI Fallout: Air Force Scraps Course That Used Videos of Tuskegee Airmen and Female WWII Pilots," *Associated Press*, January 26, 2025, https://apnews.com/article/air-force-dei-tuskegee-women-wwii-pilots-ecdeac68dc7696535d093c7690ab73bc; Stephen Losey, "Air Force Reinstates Course with Tuskegee Airmen Video After Outcry," *Air Force Times*, January 27, 2025, www.airforcetimes.com/news/your-air-force/2025/01/27/air-force-reinstates-course-with-tuskegee-airmen-video-after-outcry.

[29]Michelle Alexander, *The New Jim Crow: Mass Incarceration in the Age of Colorblindness* (New York: New Press, 2011), 7.

2. THE FEAR OF A BLACK CHILD

[1]Malcolm X, "The Most Disrespected Person in America Is the Black Woman," speech delivered in Los Angeles, California on May 22, 1962, Speakola, https://speakola.com/political/malcolm-x-speech-to-black-women-1962.

[2]Robert D. Crutchfield and Tim Wadsworth, "Poverty and Violence," in *International Handbook of Violence Research*, ed. Wilhelm Heitmeyer and John Hagan (Boston, MA: Kluwer, 2003), 67-72.

[3]Crutchfield and Wadsworth, "Poverty and Violence," 67-78.

[4]Equal Justice Initiative, "Nixon Adviser Admits War on Drugs Was Designed to Criminalize Black People," March 25, 2016, https://eji.org/news/nixon-war-on-drugs-designed-to-criminalize-Black-people.

[5]Dan Baum, "Legalize It All," *Harper's Magazine*, March 31, 2016, https://harpers.org/archive/2016/04/legalize-it-all.

[6]Baum, "Legalize It All," 2016.

[7]Michelle Alexander, "The New Jim Crow," *Ohio State Journal of Criminal Law* 9 (2011): 7.

[8]Donovan X. Ramsey, "Why the Crack Cocaine Epidemic Hit Black Communities 'First and Worst,'" interview by Tonya Mosley, WBUR, July 13, 2023, www.wbur.org/npr/1186778651/crack-cocaine-epidemic-when-crack-was-king-donovan-x-ramsey.

[9]Camille Gear Rich, "Reclaiming the Welfare Queen: Feminist and Critical Race Theory Alternatives to Existing Anti-Poverty Discourse," *Southern California Interdisciplinary Law Journal* 25, no. 2 (Spring, 2016): 257.

[10]Martin Luther King Jr., "I Have a Dream," transcript of speech delivered at the March on Washington for Jobs and Freedom, Washington, DC, August 28, 1963, https://artsandculture.google.com/asset/speech-i-have-a-dream/TwEppFBecI2Tpg.

[11]Alytia A. Levendosky et al., "Trauma Symptoms in Preschool-Age Children Exposed to Domestic Violence," *Journal of Interpersonal Violence* 17, no. 2 (February 2002): 150-64.

[12]Levendosky et al., "Trauma Symptoms," 150-53.

[13]National Institute of Mental Health, "Post-Traumatic Stress Disorder (PTSD)," revised 2023, www.nimh.nih.gov/health/publications/post-traumatic-stress-disorder-ptsd.

[14]Coreen Knowles, "More Than Adversity: Poverty as a Source of Potential Trauma in Children and Adolescents," (master's thesis, Sarah Lawrence College, 2018), 24, https://digitalcommons.slc.edu/child_development_etd/24.

[15]Joy DeGruy, *Post Traumatic Slave Syndrome: America's Legacy of Enduring Injury and Healing* (Milwaukie, OR: Uptone Press, 2005).

[16]Max Grönert, "Transgenerational Trauma—Violence Is Inherited," Medical Mondiale, accessed June 26, 2024, https://medicamondiale.org/en/violence-against-women/overcoming-trauma/transgenerational-trauma; DeGruy, *Post Traumatic Slave Syndrome*.

[17]And let me also note that during this time, it was harder to name these issues when the constant focus was on finding the best ways to exist and navigate a world filled with social exclusion and injustice.

[18]Katherine King, "What Does It Mean to Be Trauma-Informed?" *Psychology Today*, November 26, 2021, www.psychologytoday.com/ca/blog/lifespan-perspectives/202111/what-does-it-mean-be-trauma-informed.

[19]Substance Abuse and Mental Health Services Administration, *SAMHSA's Concept of Trauma and Guidance for a Trauma-Informed Approach, HHS Publication No. (SMA) 14-4884* (Rockville, MD: U.S. Department of Health and Human Services, 2014), https://library.samhsa.gov/sites/default/files/sma14-4884.pdf.

[20]R. Kirk Anderson, Brendan Landy, and Victoria Sanchez, "Trauma-Informed Pedagogy in Higher Education: Considerations for the Future of Research and Practice," *Journal of Trauma Studies in Education* 2 (2023): 125-40, https://journals.library.appstate.edu/index.php/JTSE/article/view/212; Darryl W. Stephens, "Trauma-Informed Pedagogy for the Religious and Theological Higher Education Classroom," *Religions* 11 (no. 9): 449, https://doi.org/10.3390/rel11090449.

3. AIN'T GOT NO PENCIL

[1]The Ben Hill Recreation Center was renamed and is now the William Walker Recreation Center.

[2]William J. Barber, II (@RevDrBarber), "When 7 people died from vaping, it became a White House & congressional issue. Yet, when 800 people die per day from poverty and low wealth, we hear nothing," X (formerly Twitter), March 8, 2024, 5:35 p.m., https://x.com/RevDrBarber/status/17662311883 96535957; William J. Barber, II (@RevDrBarber), "Poverty should not be a death sentence. 800 people die each day from being poor or low-wealth. We need a #ThirdReconstruction agenda that can end poverty," X (formerly Twitter), February 25, 2024, 7:14 p.m., https://x.com/RevDrBarber /status/1761907588566835465.

[3]Rev. Dr. William J. Barber II, "Rev. Dr. William J. Barber, II Speaks @ Earlham College," The Theology Network, April 6, 2024, YouTube video, 1:07:20, https:// youtu.be/x24gm1T2Aqk?si=ClZuwoLza9YuwG2x.

[4]Shailly Gupta Barnes and Saurav Sarkar, eds., *The Souls of Poor Folk: Auditing America 50 Years After the Poor People's Campaign Challenged Racism, Poverty, the War Economy/Militarism and Our National Morality* (Washington, DC: Institute for Policy Studies, 2018), 2-66; David Danelski, "Poverty is the 4th Greatest Cause of U.S. Deaths," *UCRiverside News*, April 17, 2023, https:// news.ucr.edu/articles/2023/04/17/poverty-4th-greatest-cause-us-deaths; Reverend William Barber and Gregg Gonsalves, "The Fourth Leading Cause of Death in the US? Cumulative Poverty," *The Guardian*, June 22, 2023, www .theguardian.com/commentisfree/2023/jun/22/us-leading-cause-death -poverty-crisis.

[5]Barnes and Sarkar, *The Souls of Poor Folk*, 2-115.

[6]Coreen Knowles, "More Than Adversity: Poverty as a Source of Potential Trauma in Children and Adolescents" (master's thesis, Sarah Lawrence College, 2018), https://digitalcommons.slc.edu/child_development_etd/24.

[7]Bettina M. Beech et al., "Poverty, Racism, and the Public Health Crisis in America," *Frontiers in Public Health* 9 (September 5, 2021), https://doi.org /10.3389/fpubh.2021.699049.

[8]Terence Lester, *I See You: How Love Opens Our Eyes to Invisible People* (Downers Grove, IL: InterVarsity Press, 2019), 11.

[9]Joan L. Luby, John N. Constantino, and Deanna M. Barch, "Poverty and Developing Brain," *Cerebrum* (2022), cer-04-22, www.ncbi.nlm.nih.gov/pmc /articles/PMC9224364.

[10]Kevin Johnson, "Chronic Poverty: The Implications of Bullying, Trauma, and the Education of the Poverty-Stricken Population," *European Journal of Educational Sciences*, spec. ed. (2019): 77.

[11]Coretta Scott King, "Violence has many forms," Facebook, October 19, 2023, https://m.facebook.com/photo.php?fbid=801608618638696&set=a.1303885 05760714&type=3. A picture of Coretta Scott King and the quote on her Facebook social media page, managed by The King Center.

[12]Knowles, "More Than Adversity."

[13]Take the ACES Quiz," American Society for the Positive Care of Children, accessed July 8, 2024, https://americanspcc.org/take-the-aces-quiz.

[14]"Take the ACES Quiz."

[15]Melissa T. Merrick et al., "Unpacking the Impact of Adverse Childhood Experiences on Adult Mental Health," *Child Abuse & Neglect* 69 (2017): 10-19, https://doi.org/10.1016/j.chiabu.2017.03.016.

[16]Jerome Lubbe, DC, DACNB, in conversation with the author, April 2024.

[17]Jenny Zhen-Duan, Daniella Colombo, and Kiara Alvarez, "Inclusion of Expanded Adverse Childhood Experiences in Research About Racial/Ethnic Substance Use Disparities," *American Journal of Public Health* 113, no. 52 (June 2023): S129-S132, https://doi.org/10.2105/AJPH.2023.307220.

[18]"The History of the Original ACEs Study," Project EVERS, accessed June 21, 2024, www.projectevers.org/_files/ugd/65faa0_6cb3bf6bce0a4c49803fc714d 23a0e62.pdf?index=true.

[19]Zhen-Duan, Colombo, and Alvarez, "Inclusion of Expanded Adverse Childhood Experiences."

[20]Yahoo News Australia, "The Truth Behind This Student's Viral 'I Ain't Got a Pencil' Poem," *Yahoo! News*, February 14, 2018, https://au.news.yahoo.com /the-truth-behind-this-students-viral-i-aint-got-a-pencil-poem-38953919.html.

[21]Joshua T. Dickerson, "Cause I Ain't Got a Pencil," Protective Behaviors Association, accessed June 25, 2024, www.protectivebehaviours.org/protective -behaviours-resources-training-room/poems/130-cause-i-aint-got-a-pencil. Used by permission.

4. DROPOUT BY DESIGN?

[1]James C. Howell and John P. Moore, "History of Street Gangs in the United States," *National Gang Center Bulletin,* no. 4, May 2010.

[2]Howell and Moore, "History of Street Gangs."

[3]Anthony A. Mestas, "There's a Link between Poverty and Gang Participation, but Other Factors, Too," *Pueblo Chieftain*, August 20, 2018, www.chieftain .com/story/news/2018/08/20/there-s-link-between-poverty/9384402007.

[4]Jawanza Kunjufu, *Countering the Conspiracy to Destroy Black Boys* (Chicago: African American Images, 1985).

[5]Michelle Alexander, *The New Jim Crow: Mass Incarceration in the Age of Color-blindness* (New York: New Press, 2010).

[6]Jawanza Kunjufu, "Countering the Conspiracy to Destroy Black Boys (1987)," Reelblack One, March 15, 2021, YouTube video, 55:57, www.youtube.com/watch?v=_Qgw0r29GYw.

[7]J. Hale-Benson, ed., Conference on the Black Family Proceedings, Case Western Reserve University, Cleveland, Ohio, September 25-28, 1985; Kunjufu, *The Conspiracy to Destroy Black Boys*, 20.

[8]Farima Pour-Khorshid, "Y(our) Pain Matters: Toward Healing and Abolition," TEDx talks, May 20, 2022, 0:23 to 1:13, www.youtube.com/watch?v=lKWfxMFNZFw.

[9]"New Report Finds 'Educational Redlining' Penalizes Borrowers Who Attended Community Colleges and Minority-Serving Institutions, Perpetuates Systemic Disparities," Student Borrower Protection Center, February 5. 2020, https://protectborrowers.org/new-report-finds-educational-redlining-penalizes-borrowers-who-attended-community-colleges-and-minority-serving-institutions-perpetuates-systemic-disparities/.

[10]Nadia Lathan, "50 Years after Being Outlawed, Redlining Still Drives Neighborhood Health Inequities," Berkeley Public Health, September 29, 2023, https://publichealth.berkeley.edu/news-media/research-highlights/50-years-after-being-outlawed-redlining-still-drives-neighborhood-health-inequities.

[11]Ta-Nehisi Coates, "The Case for Reparations," *The Atlantic*, June 2014, www.theatlantic.com/magazine/archive/2014/06/the-case-for-reparations/361631.

[12]Coates, "The Case for Reparations."

[13]Richard Rothstein, *The Color of Law* (New York: Liveright Publishing Corporation, 2018), 7-17.

[14]Rothstein, *Color of Law*, 18-30, 32-51, 108-30.

[15]Rothstein, *Color of Law*, 19-30.

[16]Rothstein, *Color of Law*.

[17]Rothstein, *Color of Law*, 16.

[18]Cory Turner et al., "Why America's Schools Have a Money Problem," NPR, April 18, 2016, www.npr.org/2016/04/18/474256366/why-americas-schools-have-a-money-problem.

[19]Sara Weissman, "Black Scientists with STEM PhDs Face Deep Disparities," *Inside Higher Ed.*, November 27, 2023, www.insidehighered.com/news

/diversity/race-ethnicity/2023/11/27/new-report-finds-disparities-black
-stem-phds.

20Ronald E. Butchart, "Freedman's Education in Virginia, 1861–1870," *Encyclo-pedia Virginia*, Virginia Humanities, 2020, https://encyclopediavirginia.org
/entries/freedmens-education-in-virginia-1861-1870; Library of Congress,
"Brown v. Board at Fifty: 'With an Even Hand.' A Century of Racial Segre-gation, 1849–1950," accessed July 17, 2024, www.loc.gov/exhibits/brown
/brown-segregation.html.

21Library of Congress, "Brown v. Board at Fifty."

22"Illegal to Teach Slaves to Read and Write," *Harper's Weekly*, June 21,
1862, www.sonofthesouth.net/leefoundation/civil-war/1862/june/slaves
-read-write.htm.

23Bettina L. Love, *Punished for Dreaming: How School Reform Harms Black Children
and How We Heal* (New York: St. Martin's, 2023), 7-8; Joseph Thompson, "GI
Bill Opened Doors to College for Many Vets, but Politicians Created a Separate
One for Blacks," The Conversation, March 21, 2020, https://theconversation
.com/gi-bill-opened-doors-to-college-for-many-vets-but-politicians-created
-a-separate-one-for-Blacks-126394.

24Amelia Costigan, Keshia Garnett, and Emily Troiano, "The Impact of Structural
Racism on Black Americans," Catalyst, September 30, 2020, www.catalyst.org
/research/structural-racism-Black-americans; Love, *Punished for Dreaming*, 9.

25Love, *Punished for Dreaming*, 16.

26Robert F. Smith, "Understanding Systemic Racism in Education," November 14,
2023, https://robertsmith.com/systemic-racism-in-education.

27National Commission on Excellence in Education, "A Nation at Risk: The Im-perative for Educational Reform," *The Elementary School Journal* 84, no. 2
(1983): 112-30, www.jstor.org/stable/1001303.

28Love, *Punished for Dreaming*, 7-8.

29Love, *Punished for Dreaming*, 9.

30The school recently transitioned into The Promise Career Institute to serve
nontraditional high school students and those seeking alternative pathways
to education and career readiness. Its mission is to provide flexible, career-oriented programs that help students overcome personal, social, or academic
challenges while preparing them for success in the workforce. By focusing on
hands-on training in fields like automotive technology, cybersecurity, and lo-gistics, The Promise Career Institute ensures that students not only complete
their education but also leave with practical skills to build their future. I am
grateful that the organization I cofounded, Love Beyond Walls, was

instrumental in giving back to students like I once was at that location. Additionally, our offices are less than a mile away.

5. WITHOUT A ROOF

[1]Institute for Children, Poverty & Homelessness, "No Longer Hidden: The Health and Well-Being of Homeless High School Students," Infographic, *Health*, October 2019, www.icph.org/maps_infographics/no-longer-hidden-infographic.

[2]Deborah K. Padgett, "Homelessness, Housing Instability and Mental Health: Making the Connections," *BJPsych Bulletin* 44, no. 5 (2020): 197-201, https://doi.org/10.1192/bjb.2020.49.

[3]Ellen L. Bassuk and Steven M. Friedman, "Facts on Trauma and Homeless Children," National Child Traumatic Stress Network; Homelessness and Extreme Poverty Working Group, 2005, www.nctsn.org/sites/default/files/resources/facts_on_trauma_and_homeless_children.pdf.

[4]Radio Diaries, "The Bonus Army: How a Protest Led to the GI Bill," NPR, November 11, 2011, www.npr.org/2011/11/11/142224795/the-bonus-army-how-a-protest-led-to-the-gi-bill.

[5]Lorna Hermosura, "School-to-Prison Pipeline Is a Direct Policy Descendant of Nixon's War on Drugs," *UT News*, April 25, 2016, https://news.utexas.edu/2016/04/25/school-to-prison-pipeline-caused-by-war-on-drugs-policy.

[6]I hold nothing against those who take this nontraditional route to obtain education. However, during that time a couple of key conversations educated me to take a different route.

6. FIFTH-YEAR PERSISTER

[1]Honestly, I didn't want to succumb to the labels that society had placed on me. I had to deal with the embarrassment of not finishing on time and the lack of community support I felt I could trust as I tried to navigate my context. Also, I had just moved back in with my mother and wondered whether I would even have enough emotional strength and courage to reach my goal of finishing school.

[2]"Race, the Media and the Myth of the 'Crack Baby,'" Retro Report, PBS LearningMedia, August 23, 2021, https://gpb.pbslearningmedia.org/resource/race-media-and-the-myth-of-the-crack-baby-video/retro-report; Calvin John Smiley and David Fakunle, "From 'Brute' to 'Thug': The Demonization and Criminalization of Unarmed Black Male Victims in America," *Journal of Human Behavior in the Social Environment* 26, no. 3-4 (2016): 350-66, https://doi.org/10.1080/10911359.2015.1129256; Priyanka Boghani, "They Were Sentenced as 'Superpredators.' Who Were They Really?," PBS, May 2, 2017, www.pbs.org

/wgbh/frontline/article/they-were-sentenced-as-superpredators-who-were
-they-really.

[3]Brenda M. Morton, "Trauma and Academic Impact: Stories from At-Risk Youth," *Northwest Journal of Teacher Education* 17, no. 2 (2022): 4, https://pdx scholar.library.pdx.edu/nwjte/vol17/iss2/4.

[4]US Department of Housing and Urban Development, "Understanding Neighborhood Effects of Concentrated Poverty," *Evidence Matters* (Winter 2011), www.huduser.gov/portal/periodicals/em/winter11/highlight2.html.

[5]Lewis V. Baldwin and Vicki L. Crawford, eds., *Reclaiming the Great World House: The Global Vision of Martin Luther King Jr.* (Atlanta: University of Georgia Press, 2019), 59-75.

[6]Mathew C. Uretsky and Angela K. Henneberger, "Fifth Year Persisters: High School, College, and Early Career Outcomes for Persisting Non-Graduates," *Children and Youth Services Review* 115 (2020): 1-44, https://doi.org/10.1016/j.childyouth.2020.105058.

7. WHEN FAITH CONFRONTS TRAUMA

[1]Jessica Larché, "Data Shows Black Men Receive Harsher Punishments than Whites for Same Crimes," WTKR, February 21, 2022, www.wtkr.com/investigations/data-shows-black-men-receive-harsher-punishments-than-whites-for-same-crimes.

[2]Jennifer Rainey Marquez, "Same Crime, More Time," *Georgia State University Research Magazine* (Spring 2020), https://news.gsu.edu/research-magazine/spring2020/incarceration.

[3]M. Marit Rehavi and Sonja B. Starr, "Racial Disparity in Federal Criminal Sentences," *Journal of Political Economy* 122, no. 6 (2014): 1320-54.

[4]Jemar Tisby, "Shaken and Heartsick: Another Professor at a Christian University Fired for Racial Justice Teachings," *Footnotes by Jemar Tisby*, May 1, 2023, https://jemartisby.substack.com/p/shaken-and-heartsick-another-professor.

[5]"Banned Books by State," World Population Review, accessed July 8, 2024, https://worldpopulationreview.com/state-rankings/banned-books-by-state.

[6]Supad Kumar Ghose, "The Role of the Black Church in the American Civil Rights Movement," *UITS Journal* 5, no. 1 (2015): 58-68, https://research.uits.edu.bd/wp-content/uploads/2023/08/The-Role-of-the-Black-Church-in-the-American-Civil-Rights-Movement.pdf.

[7]Jemar Tisby, *The Spirit of Justice* (Grand Rapids, MI: Zondervan, 2024).

[8]Allison Calhoun-Brown, "Upon This Rock: The Black Church, Nonviolence, and the Civil Rights Movement," *Political Science and Politics* 33, no. 2 (2000): 168-74, https://doi.org/10.2307/420886.

[9]"About Wilberforce University," Wilberforce University, accessed June 26, 2024, https://wilberforce.edu/about-wilberforce.

[10]"Our History," Morehouse College, accessed June 26, 2024, https://more house.edu/about/our-history.

[11]"About Wilberforce University," Wilberforce University; "Our History," Morehouse College.

[12]"History," Morris Brown College, accessed June 26, 2024, https://morris brown.edu/history.

8. WORK AND WORTHINESS

[1]Martin Luther King, Jr., "The Drum Major Instinct," transcription of sermon delivered at Ebenezer Baptist Church, Atlanta, GA, on February 4, 1968, https:// bethlehemfarm.net/wp-content/uploads/2013/02/DrumMajorInstinct.pdf.

[2]"Affirmative Action," History.com, June 13, 2023, updated June 29, 2023, www .history.com/topics/us-government-and-politics/affirmative-action.

[3]Courtney Cohn, "Trump Revokes Biden's 2021 Executive Order Expanding Voting Access," Democracy Docket, January 21, 2025, www.democracydocket .com/news-alerts/trump-revokes-bidens-2021-executive-order-expanding -voting-access; "Fact Sheet: President Donald J. Trump Protects Civil Rights and Merit-Based Opportunity by Ending Illegal DEI," The White House, January 22, 2025, www.whitehouse.gov/fact-sheets/2025/01/fact-sheet -president-donald-j-trump-protects-civil-rights-and-merit-based-opportunity -by-ending-illegal-dei/.

[4]Kimberley Richards, "Trump Promoted This Disputed Racial Theory in His Inaugural Speech. Here's Why It Doesn't Work," Huffpost, January 21, 2025, www.huffpost.com/entry/donald-trump-inauguration-speech-colorbli nd_l_678fef6ee4b0b9429ede0f6f.

[5]"President Trump Revokes Executive Order 11246's Affirmative Action Re- quirements for Federal Government Contractors," Thompson Hine LLP, January 22, 2025, www.thompsonhine.com/insights/president-trump -revokes-executive-order-11246s-affirmative-action-requirements-for-federal -government-contractors/.

[6]"Affirmative Action," History.com.

[7]Andre M. Perry, Hannah Stephens, and Manann Donoghoe, "The Supreme Court's Decision to Strike Down Affirmative Action Means That HBCU

Investment Is More Important than Ever," Brookings, June 29, 2023, www
.brookings.edu/articles/the-supreme-courts-decision-to-strike-down
-affirmative-action-means-that-hbcu-investment-is-more-important-than-ever.

8Jill Barshay, "Another Way to Quantify Inequality Inside Colleges," The Hech-
inger Report, February 17, 2020, https://hechingerreport.org/another-way-to
-quantify-inequality-inside-colleges.

9Perry, Stephens, and Donoghoe, "The Supreme Court's Decision."

10Perry, Stephens, and Donoghoe, "The Supreme Court's Decision."

11I attended Atlanta Bible College, and this college was a space where I learned
about the Bible. After attending, I realized that it taught a doctrine that went
against my personal theological beliefs, but it did give me the ability to grow
closer to God in ways that were beneficial to my personal development.

9. REDEMPTION AND THE HEALING POWER OF COMMUNITY

1"Tulsa Race Massacre," Tulsa Historical Society and Museum, accessed July 8,
2024, www.tulsahistory.org/exhibit/1921-tulsa-race-massacre.

2Monica Moorehead, "U.S. Ethnic Cleansing: The 1921 Tulsa Massacre," Workers
World, June 10, 1999, www.hartford-hwp.com/archives/45a/416.html.

3"Tulsa Race Massacre."

4"Tulsa Race Massacre."

5Nicole Chavez, "Tulsa Massacre Survivor at 107 Years Old Testifies That the
Horror of That Day Never Goes Away," CNN, May 20, 2021, www.cnn.com
/2021/05/19/us/tulsa-massacre-survivors-congress/index.html.

6Alex Albright et al., "After the Burning: The Economic Effects of the 1921 Tulsa
Race Massacre," National Bureau of Economic Research Working Paper
No. 28985, June, 2021, www.nber.org/system/files/working_papers/w28985/
w28985.pdf.

7Chavez, "Tulsa Massacre Survivor at 107."

8Chavez, "Tulsa Massacre Survivor at 107."

10. SAFE SPACES AND COMEBACK STORIES

1"Our History," Simmons College of Kentucky, accessed June 12, 2024, https://
simmonscollegeky.edu/about/.

2"An Unsung Hero: Elijah Mars" [video], Shelby County Historical Society, accessed June 12, 2024, www.shelbykyhistory.org/elijah%20marrs.html.

3Howard Cabiao, "Simmons College of Kentucky (1879–)," BlackPast, December 31, 2010, www.blackpast.org/african-american-history/simmons
-college-kentucky-1879/.

[4]Cabiao, "Simmons College of Kentucky."

[5]Although it could have received this designation in 1965.

[6]Yvonne Coleman Bach, "HBCU Storyteller Spotlight: Simmons College of Kentucky," HBCUstory, March 14, 2014, http://hbcustory.org/hbcu-storyteller-spotlight-simmons-college-of-kentucky-2.

[7]"History," Union Institute & University, accessed July 2, 2024, https://myunion.edu/who-is-union-institute-university.

[8]Jonathon Gregg, "Simmons College Launches 'Open Door' Initiative to Bring Educational Opportunities to Houseless," *Spectrum News 1*, Louisville, KY, May 10, 2024, https://spectrumnews1.com/ky/louisville/news/2024/05/09/simmons-college-kentucky-louisville-open-door-initiative-; Reyna Katko, "From Struggle to Success, Simmons College Launches Effort to Study Louisville's Homeless Problem," WDRB, May 9, 2024, www.wdrb.com/news/education/from-struggle-to-success-simmons-college-launches-effort-to-study-louisvilles-homeless-problem/article_fe5a0bfe-0e2f-11ef-8fdc-1fcd51e3a782.html.

[9]Terence Lester, "The Supreme Court Declares Homelessness a Crime: A Scholarly Lament," *From Streets to Scholarship*, June 28, 2024, https://substack.com/home/post/p-146094249.

[10]"Advancing Care and Justice for the Unhoused," USC Street Medicine, Keck School of Medicine of USC, accessed May 23, 2024, https://keck.usc.edu/street-medicine.

EPILOGUE: THIS IS HAPPENING

[1]Terence Lester, "When Policy Overlooks Worth: Exploring Harmful Policies and Social Constructions That Exclude the Unhoused from Martin Luther King, Jr.'s Beloved Community" (Doctoral dissertation, The Union Institute, 2023).

[2]"Biography of Edward A. Bouchet," The Graduate School, Northwestern University, accessed August 8, 2024, www.northwestern.edu/tgs/success/retention/bouchet-honor-society/biography-of-edward-a.-bouchet.html.

ACKNOWLEDGMENTS

[1]Frederick Douglass, "West India Emancipation," transcript of speech delivered at Canandaigua, New York, August 3, 1857, https://rbscp.lib.rochester.edu/4398.